Shapes and patterns

abstract forms

a coloring book adventure

Anca Andrei

1

ISBN-13: 978-1723379710
ISBN-10: 1723379719

anca.andrei.001@gmail.com

COMPUTER GENERATED IMAGES AND PATTERNS TO COLOR....

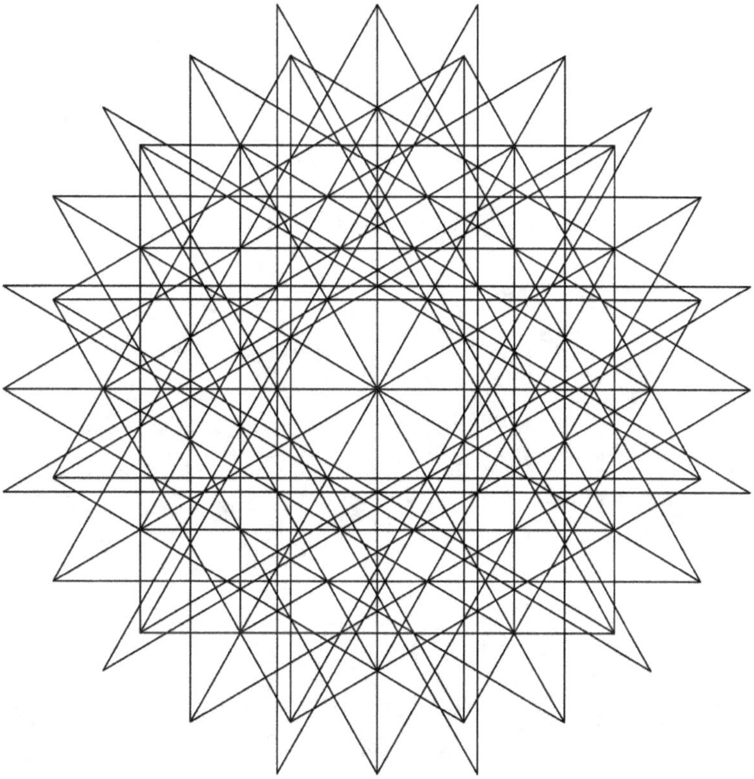

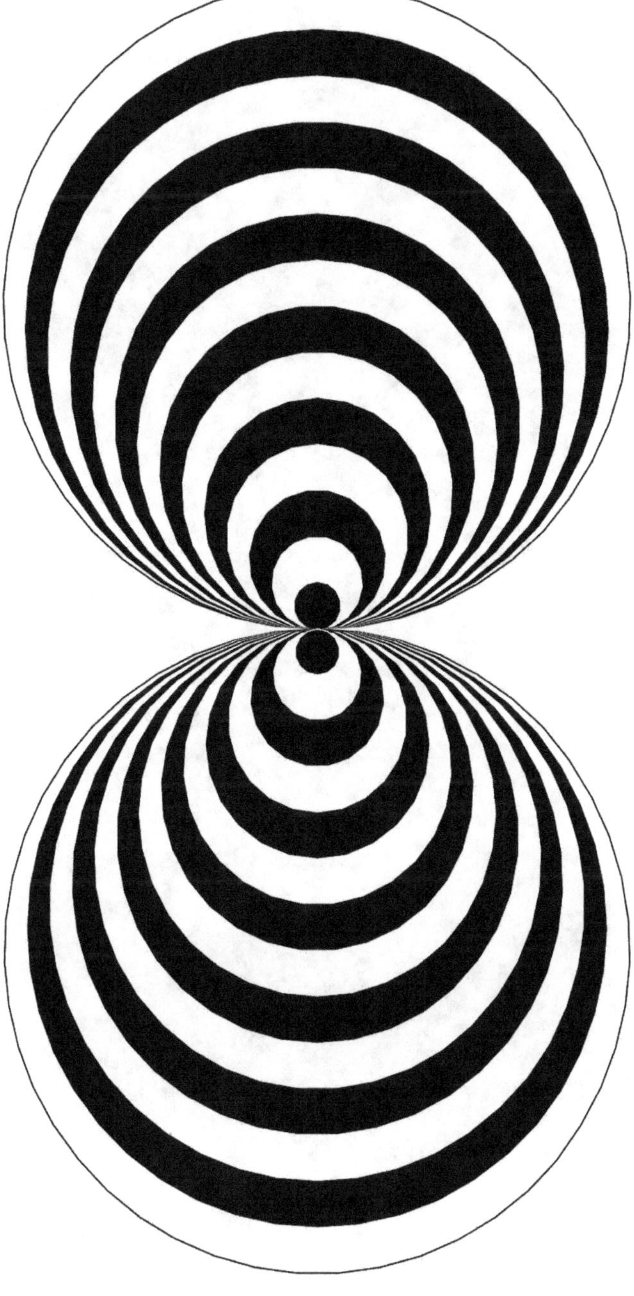

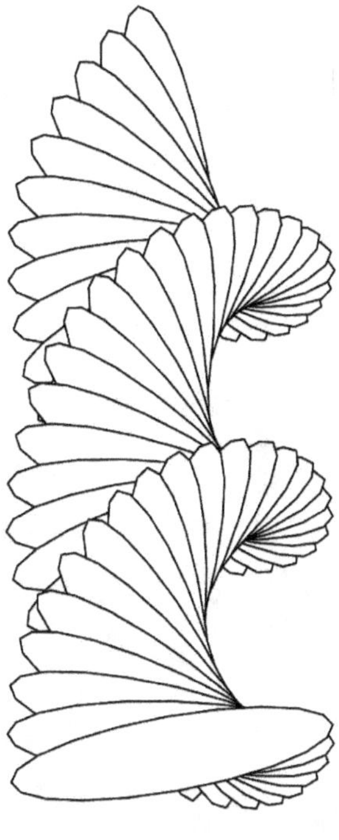

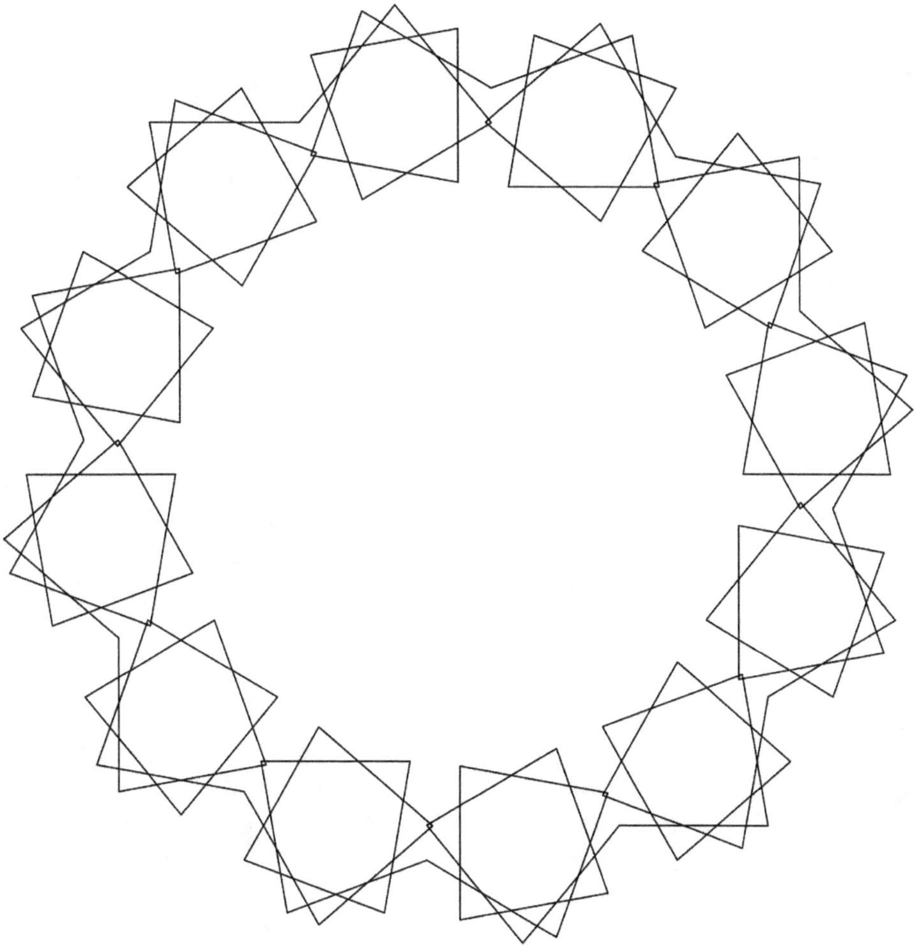

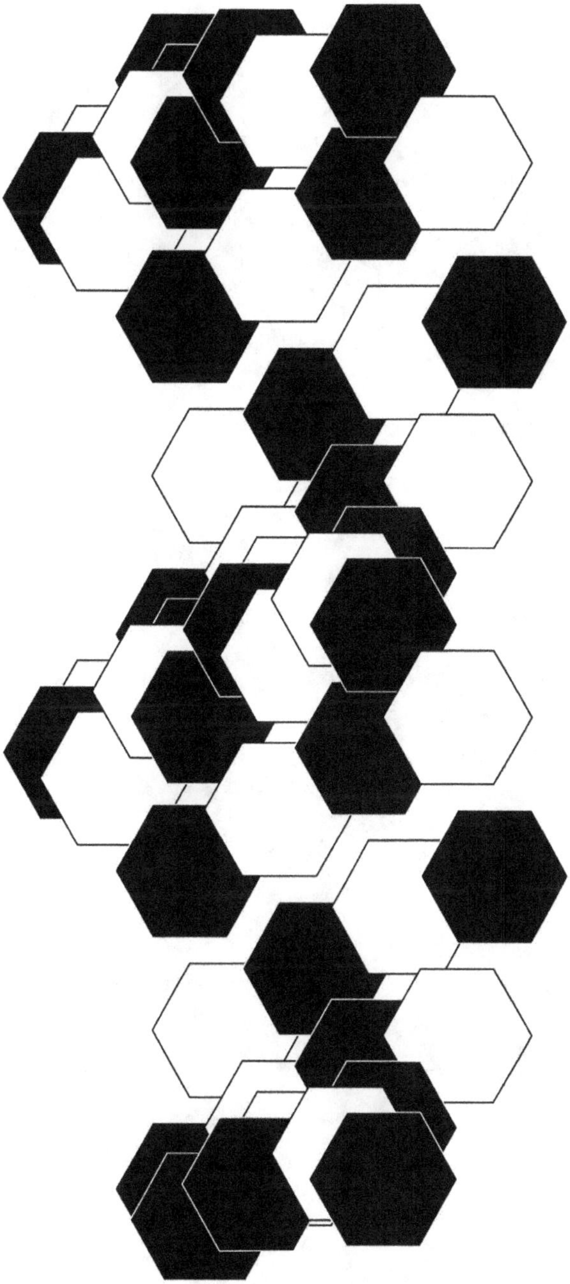

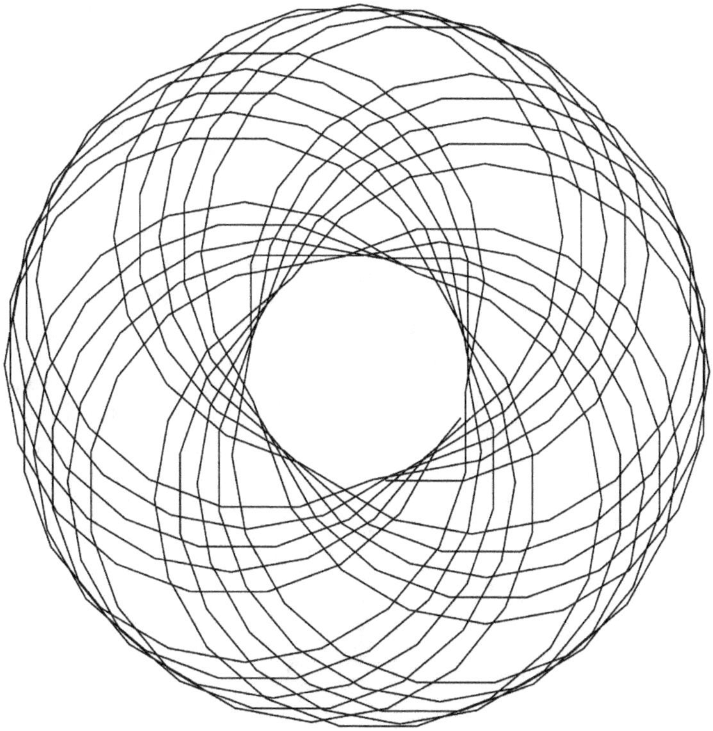

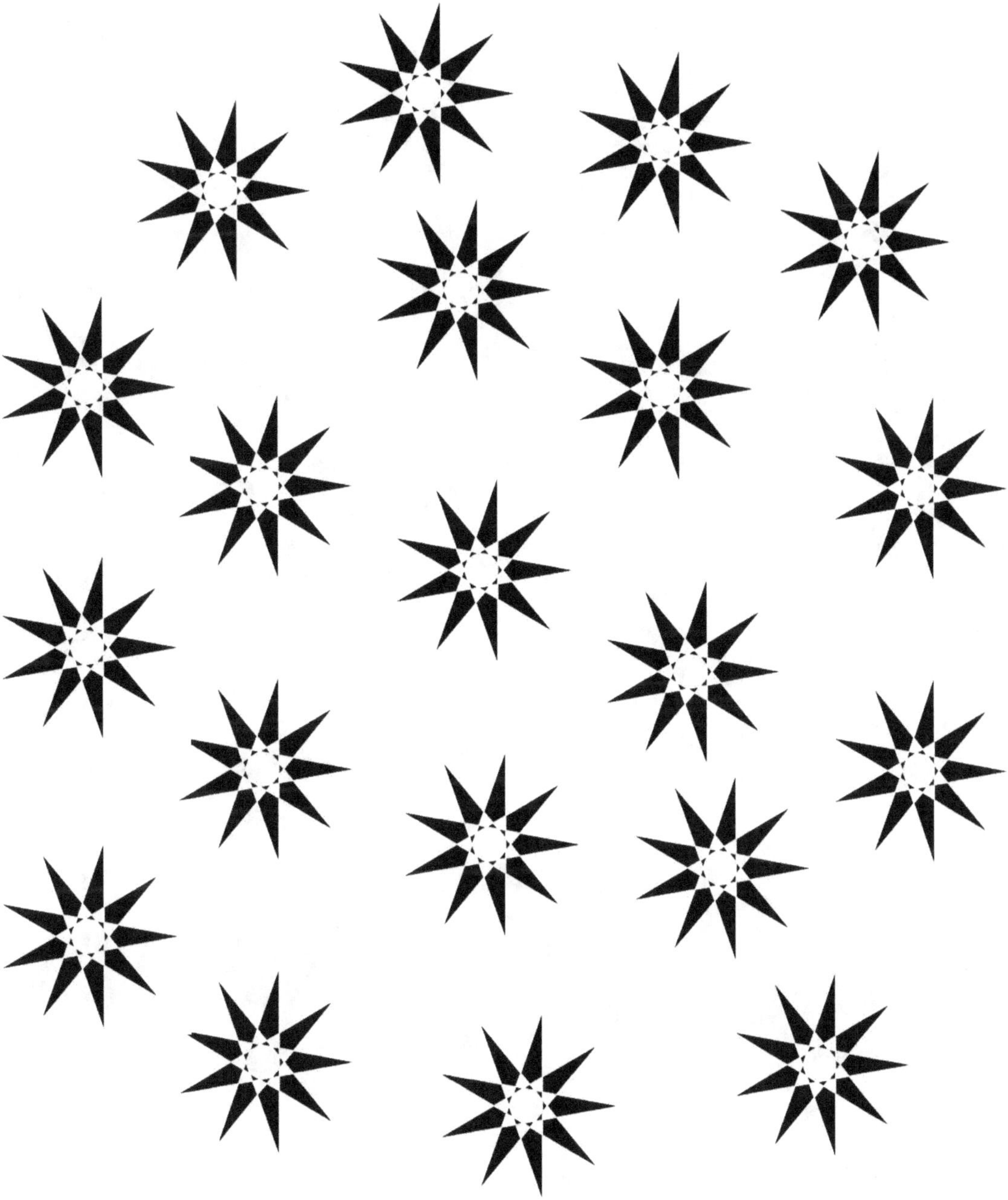

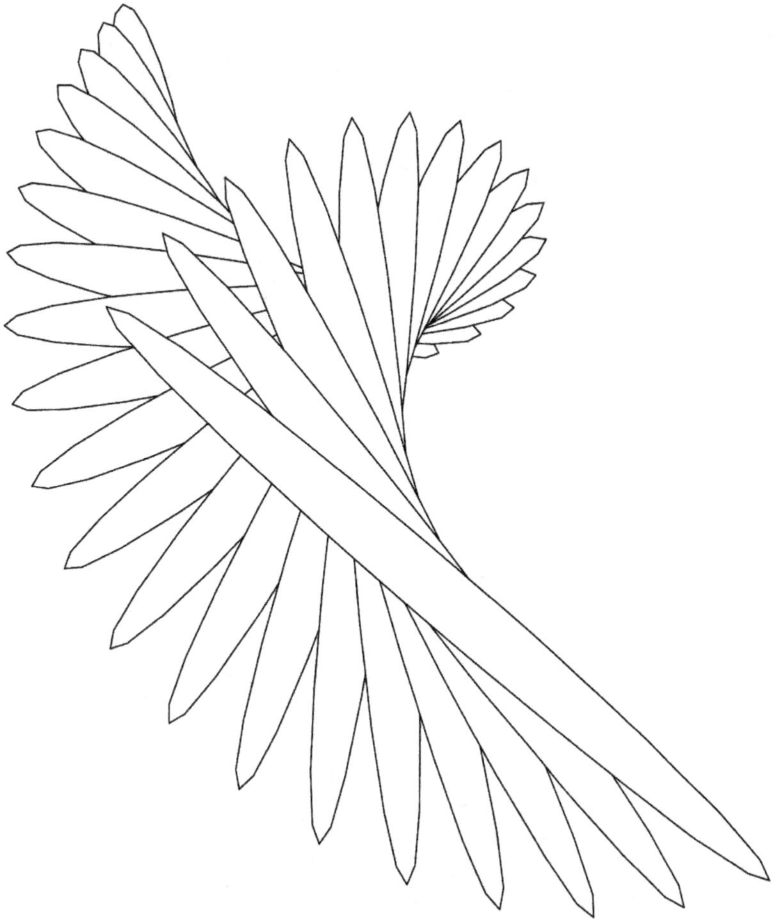

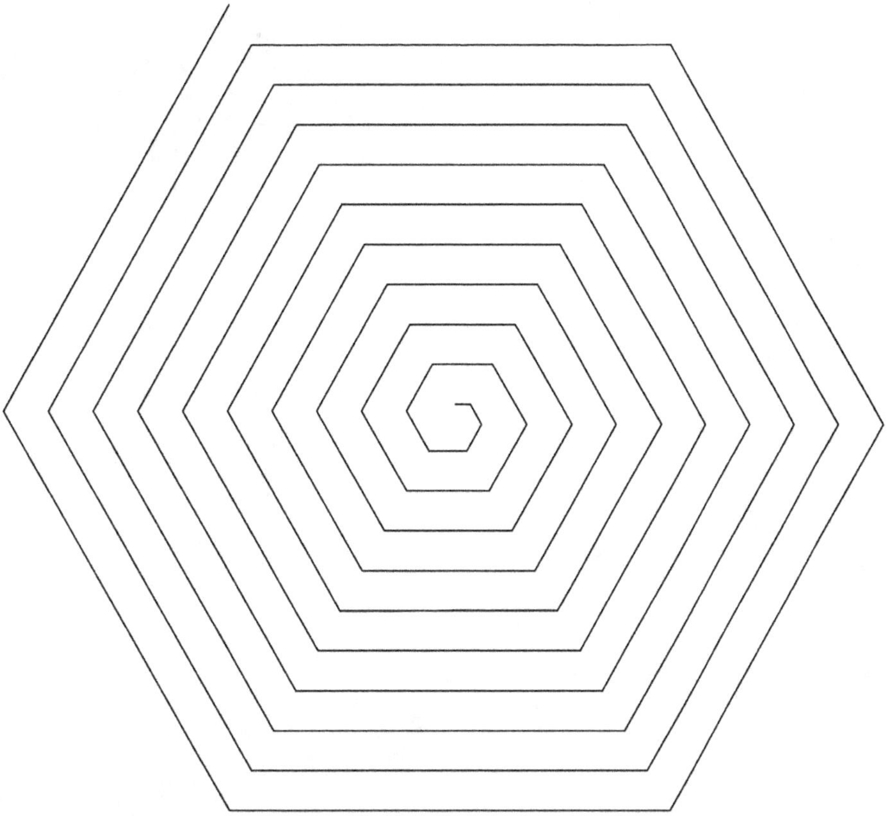

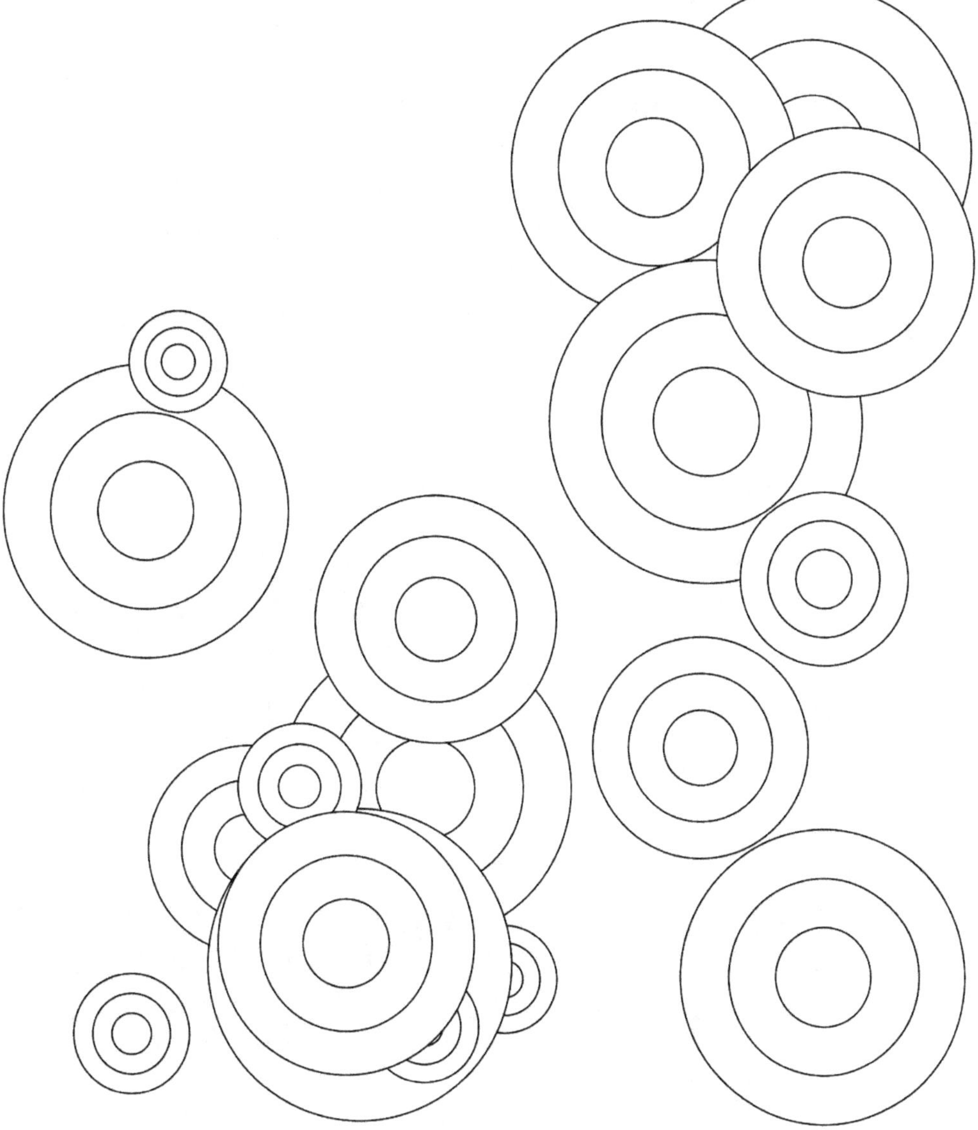

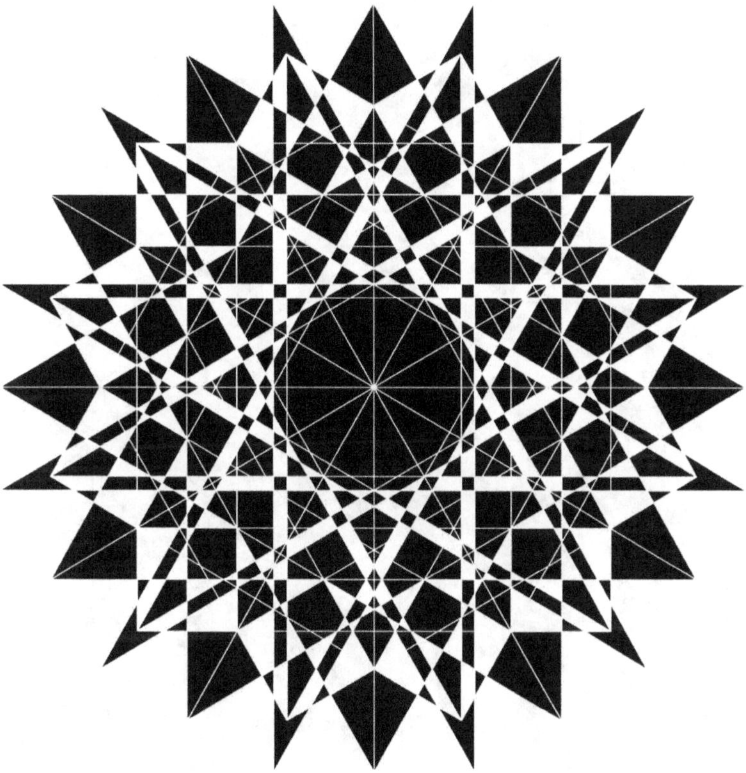

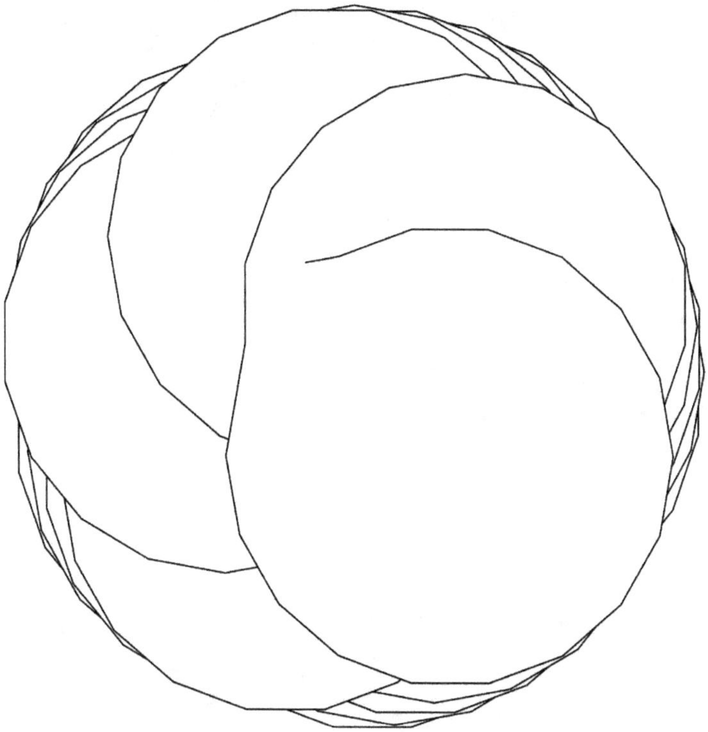

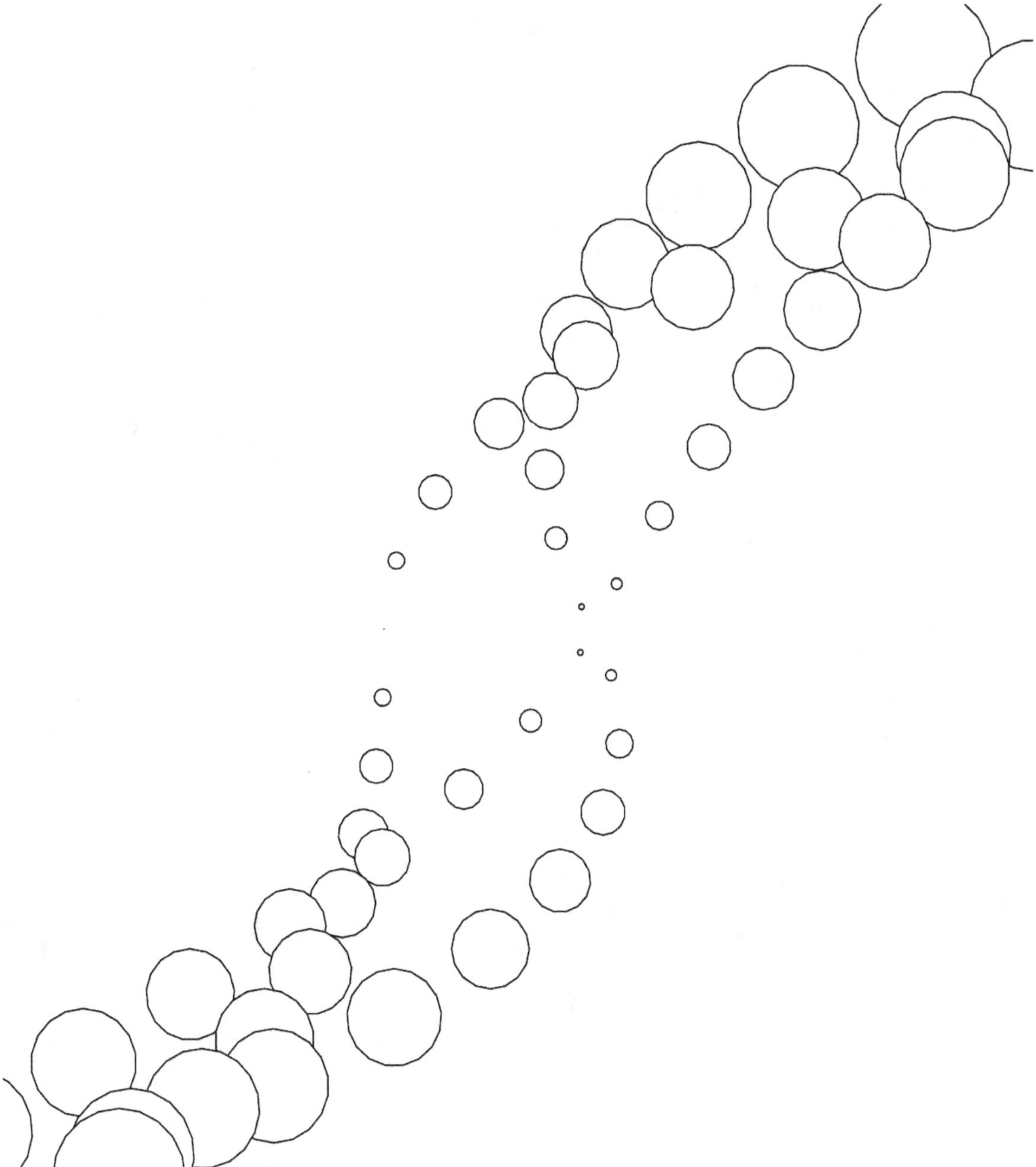

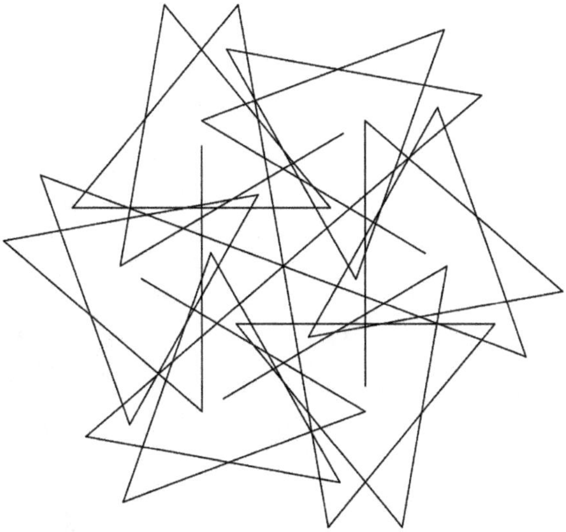

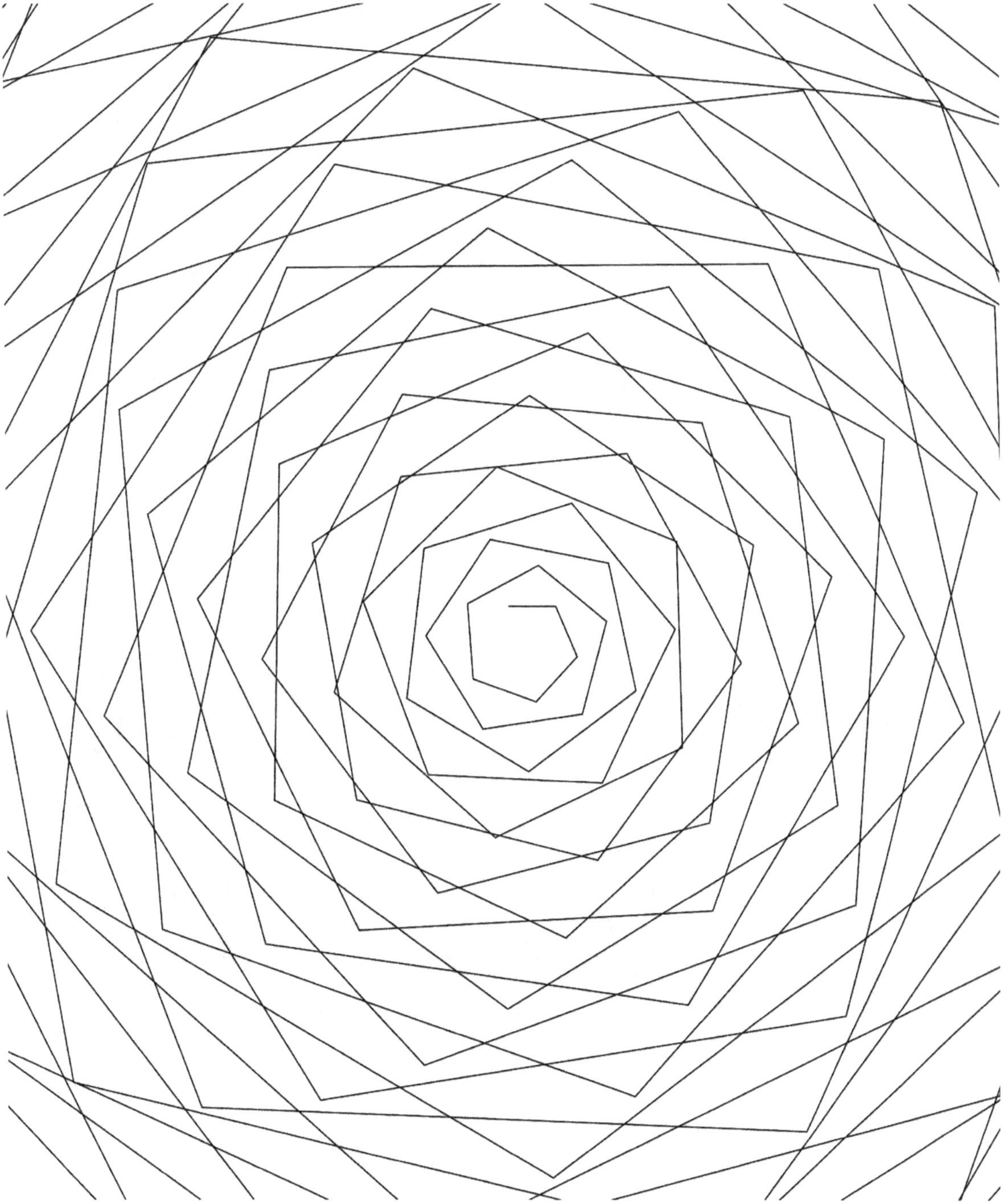

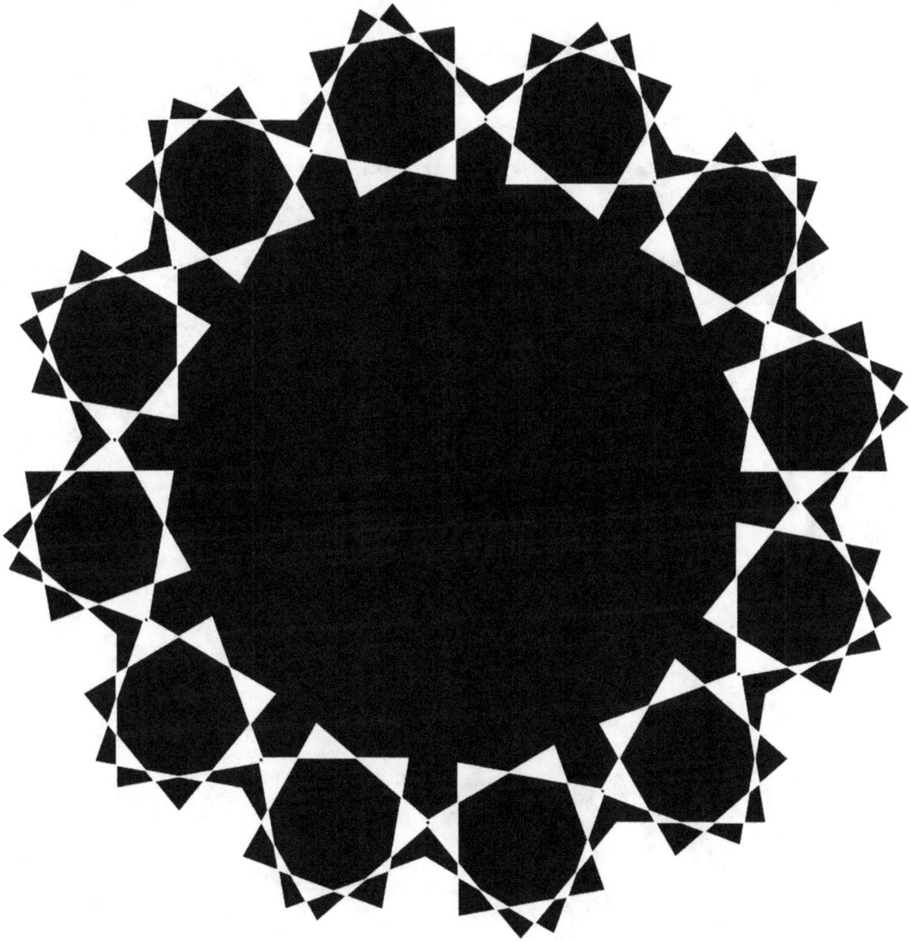

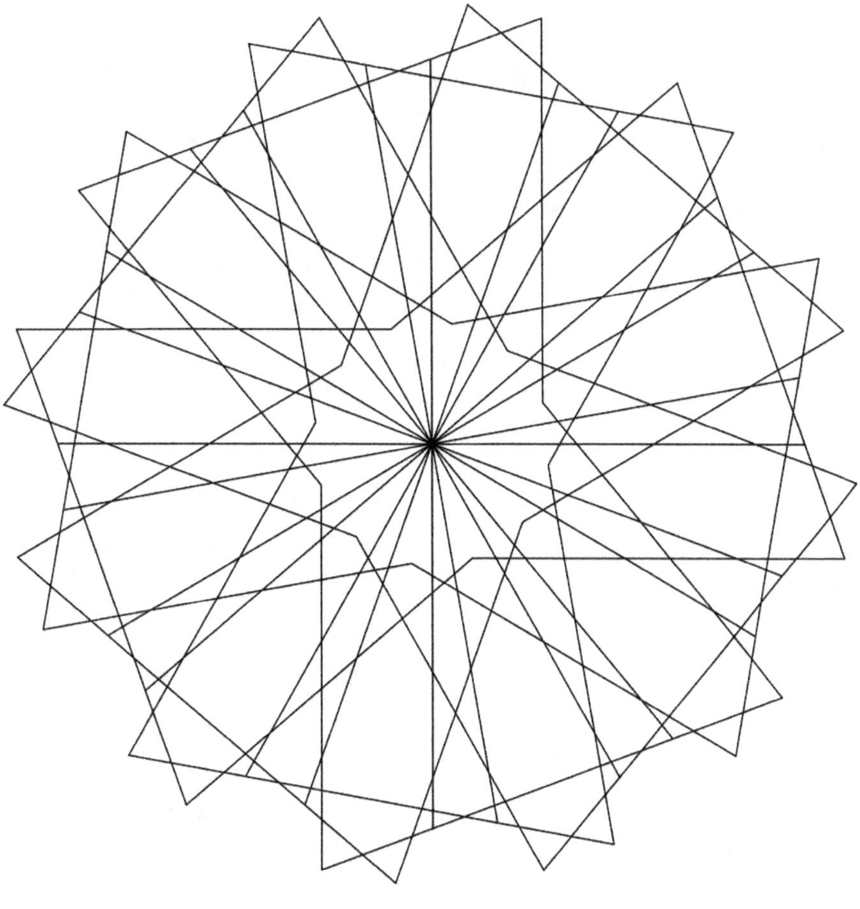

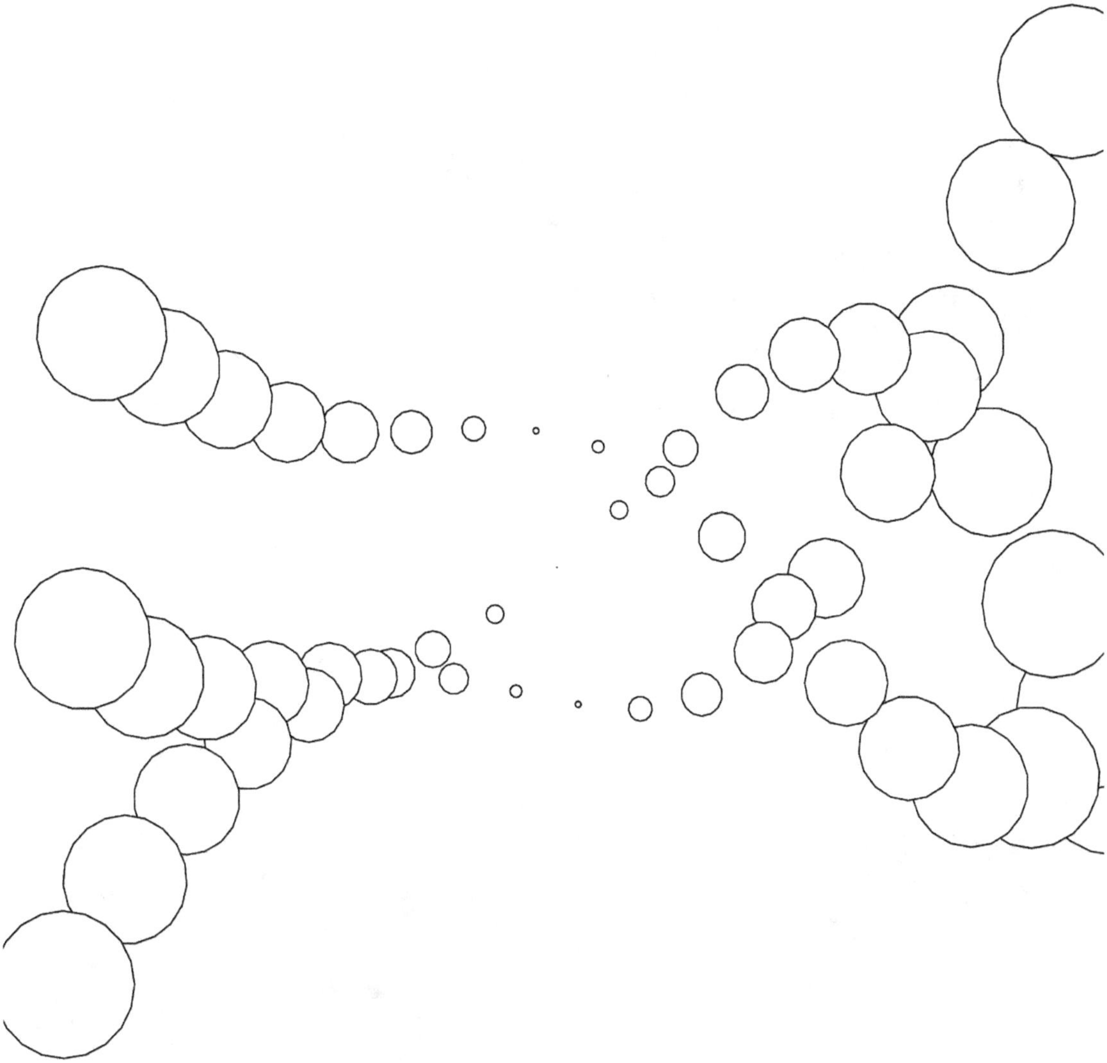

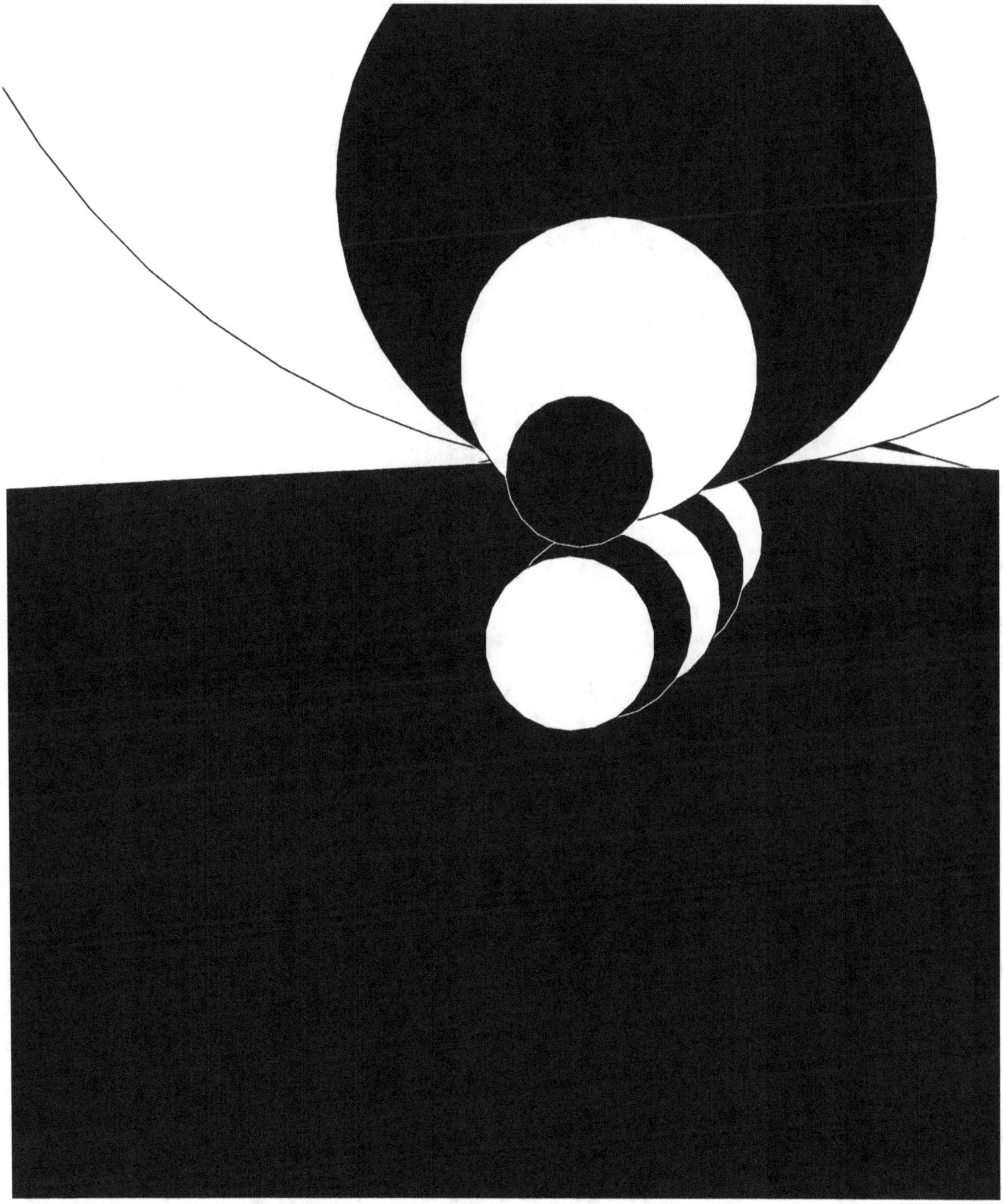

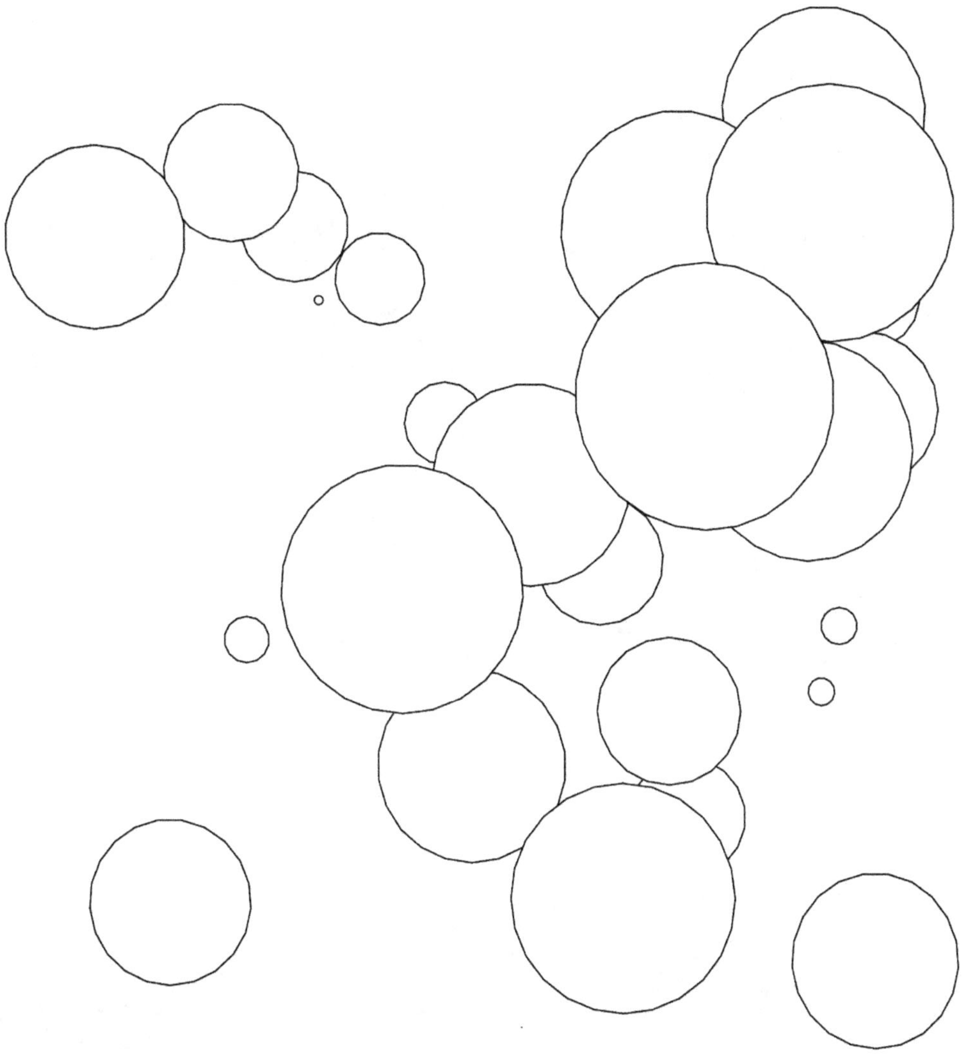

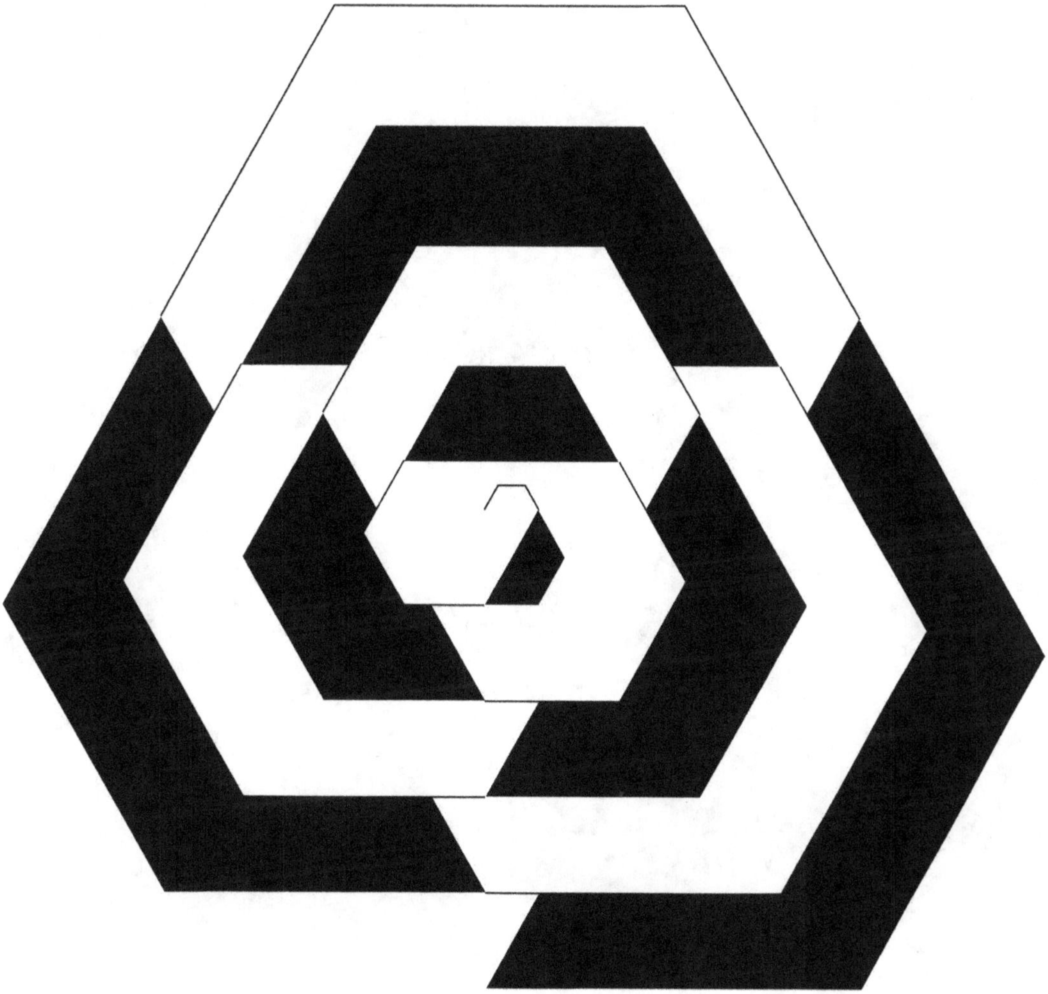

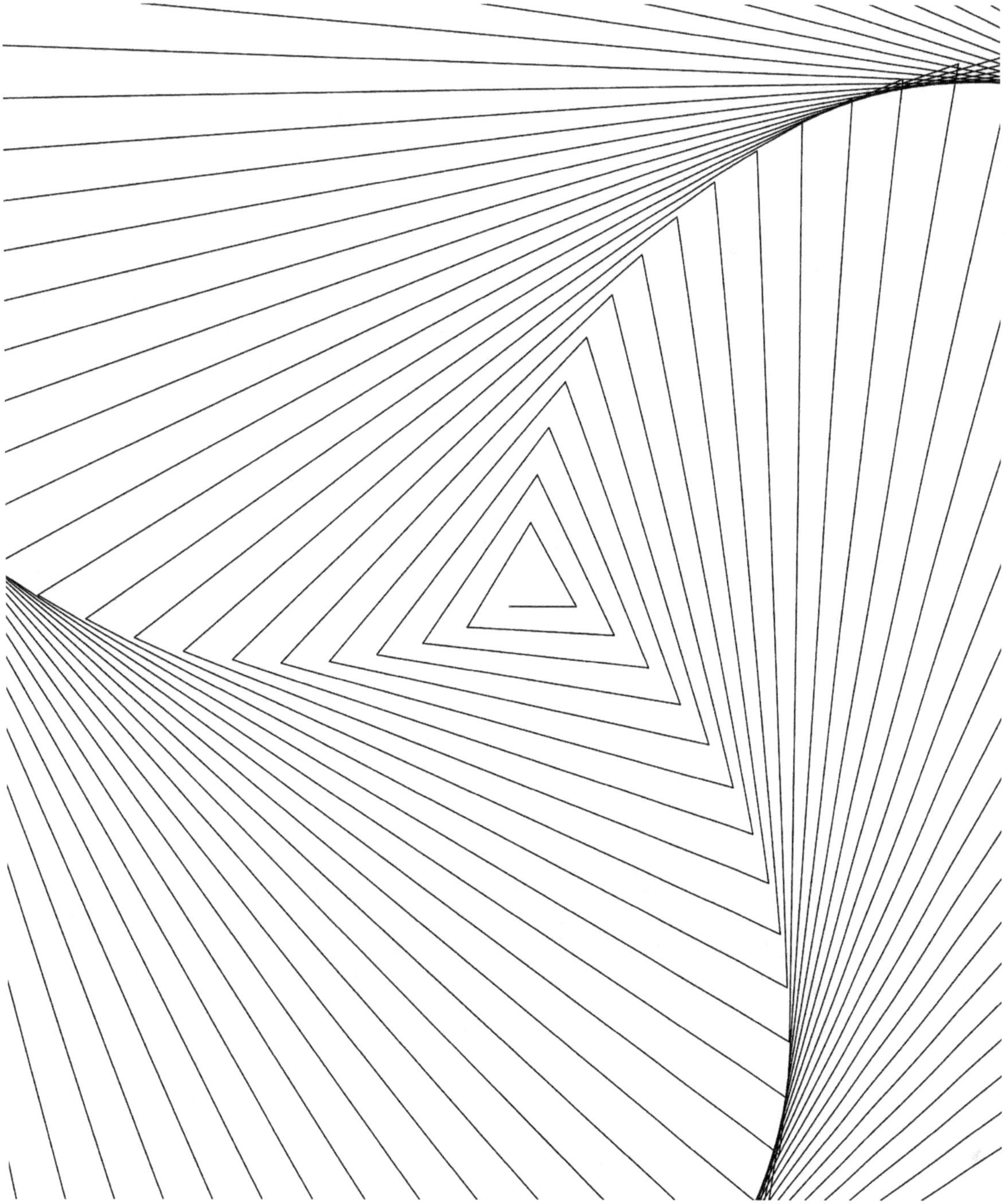

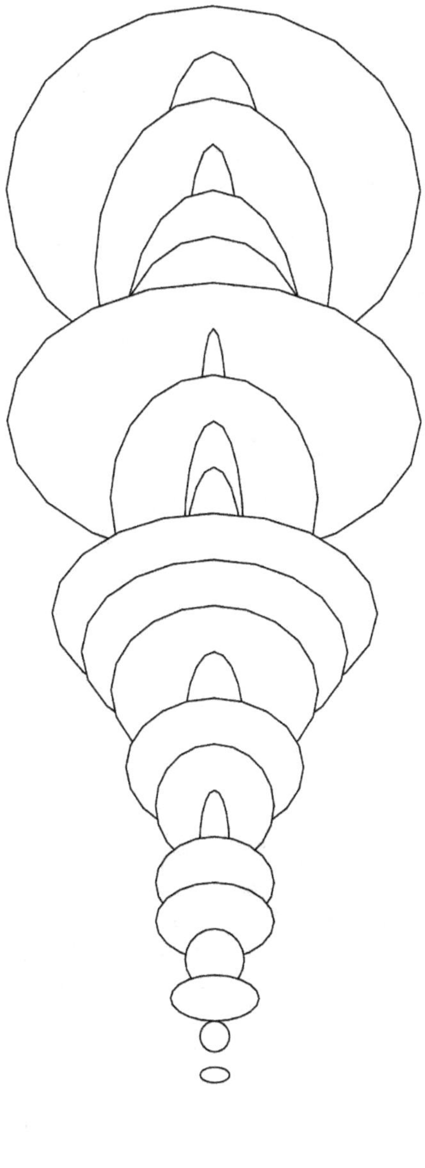

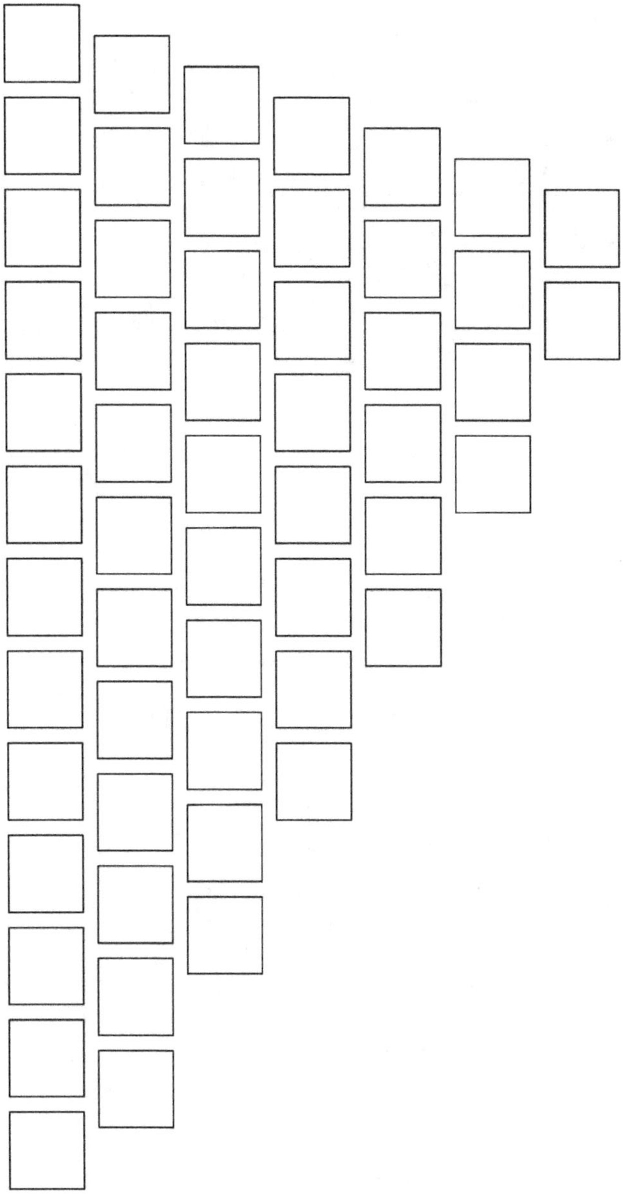

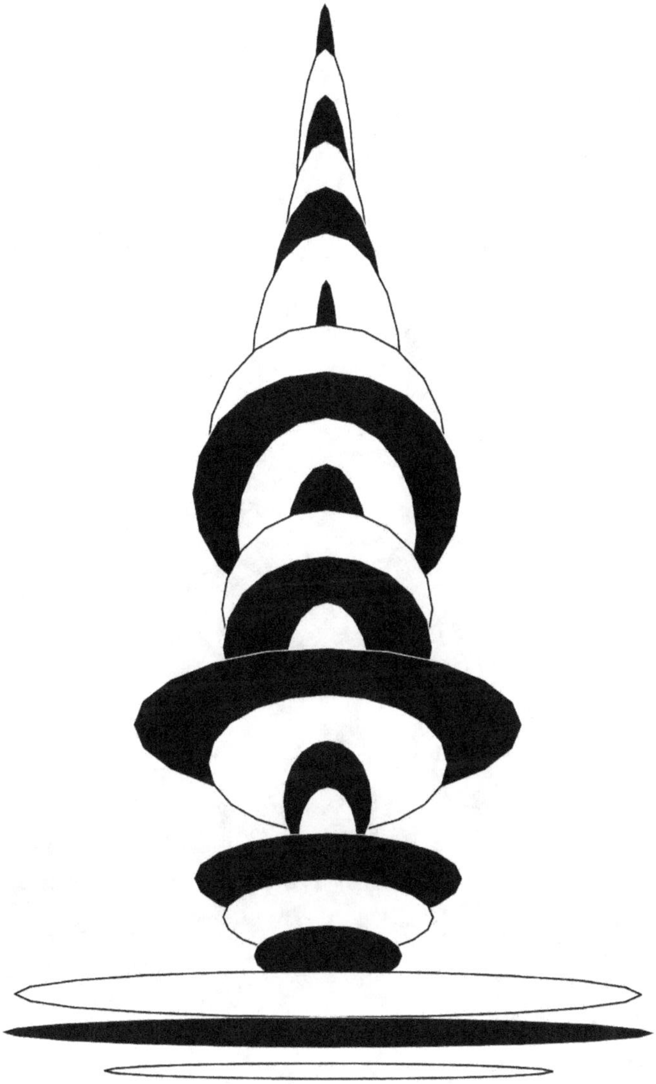

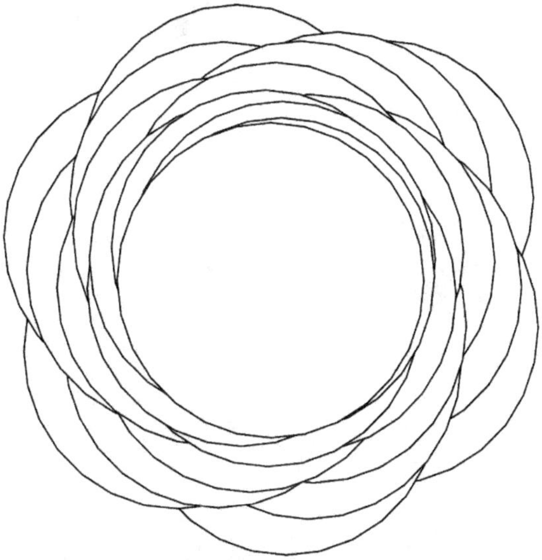

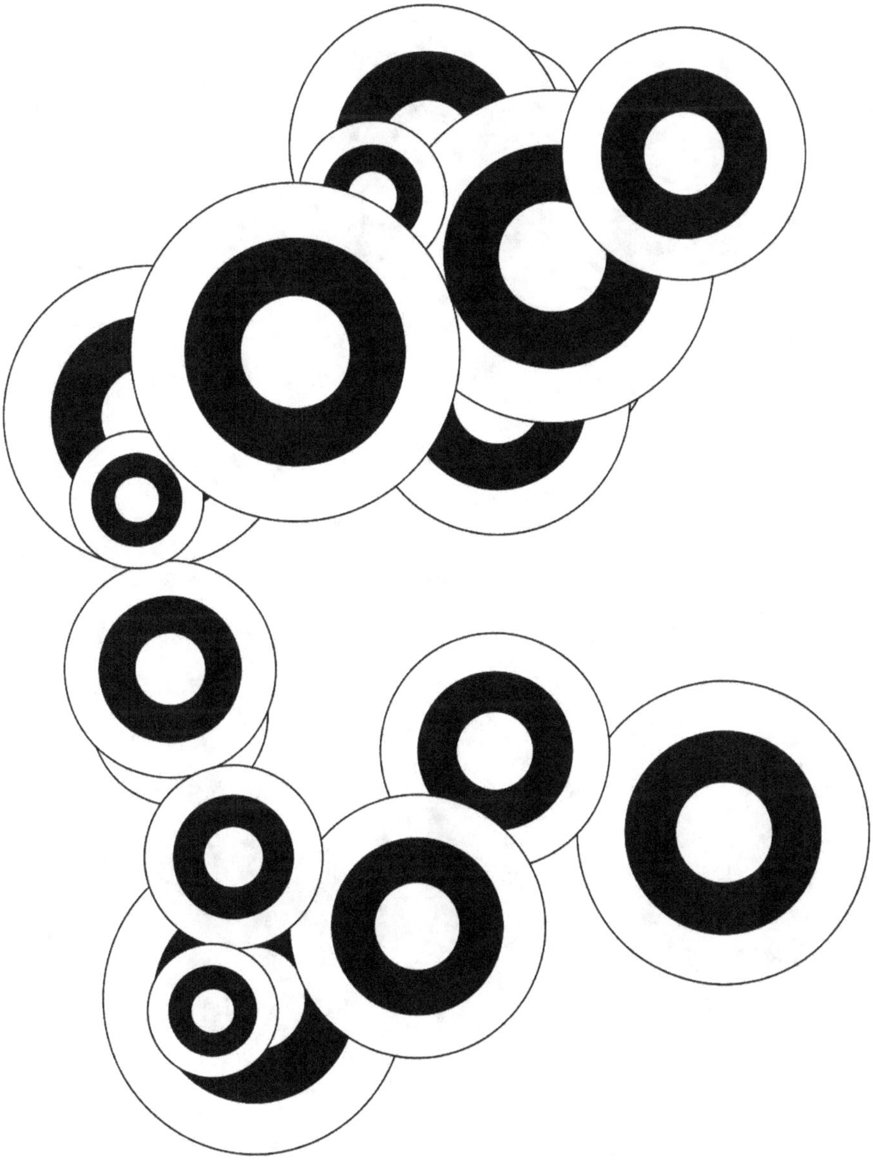

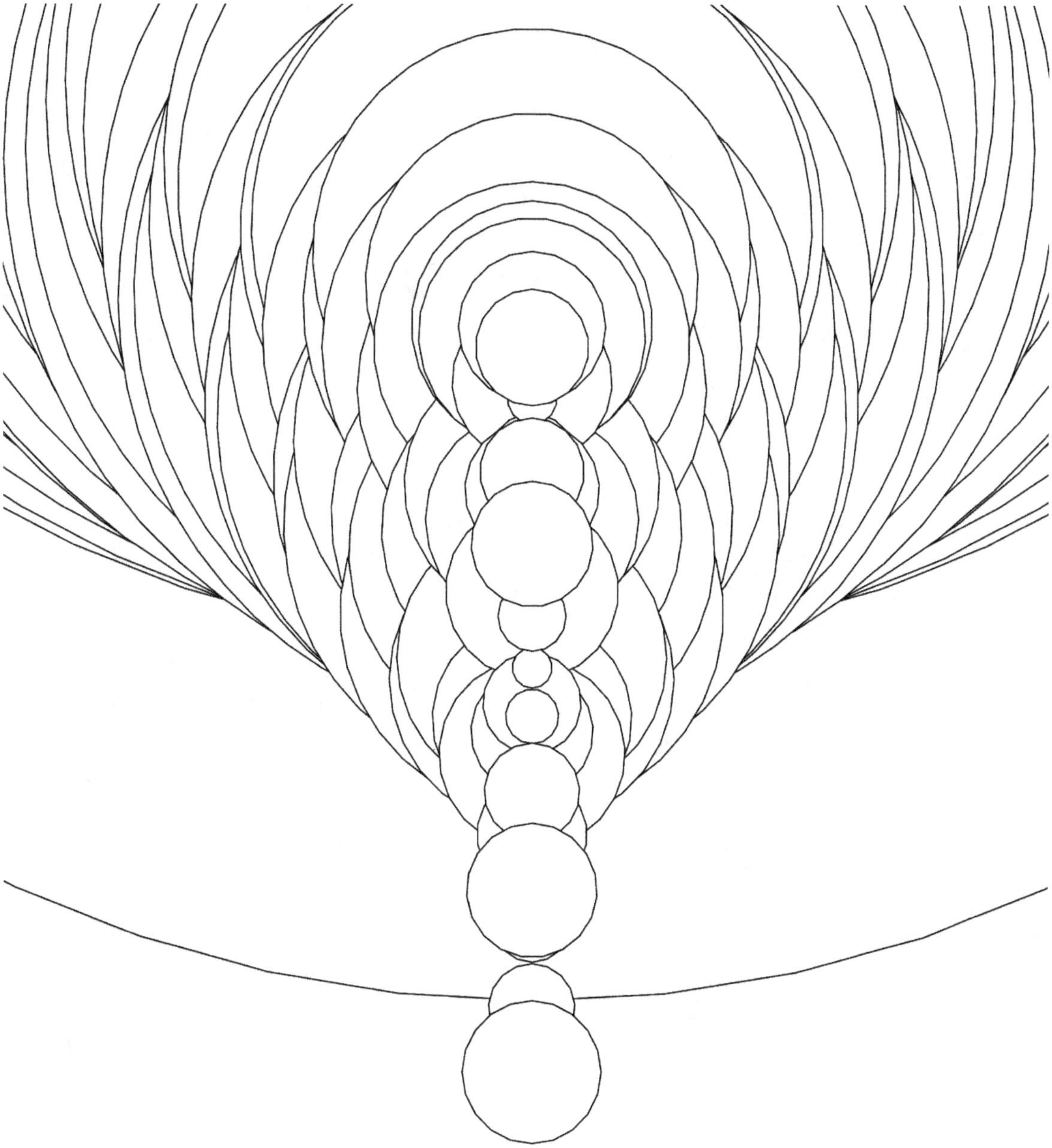

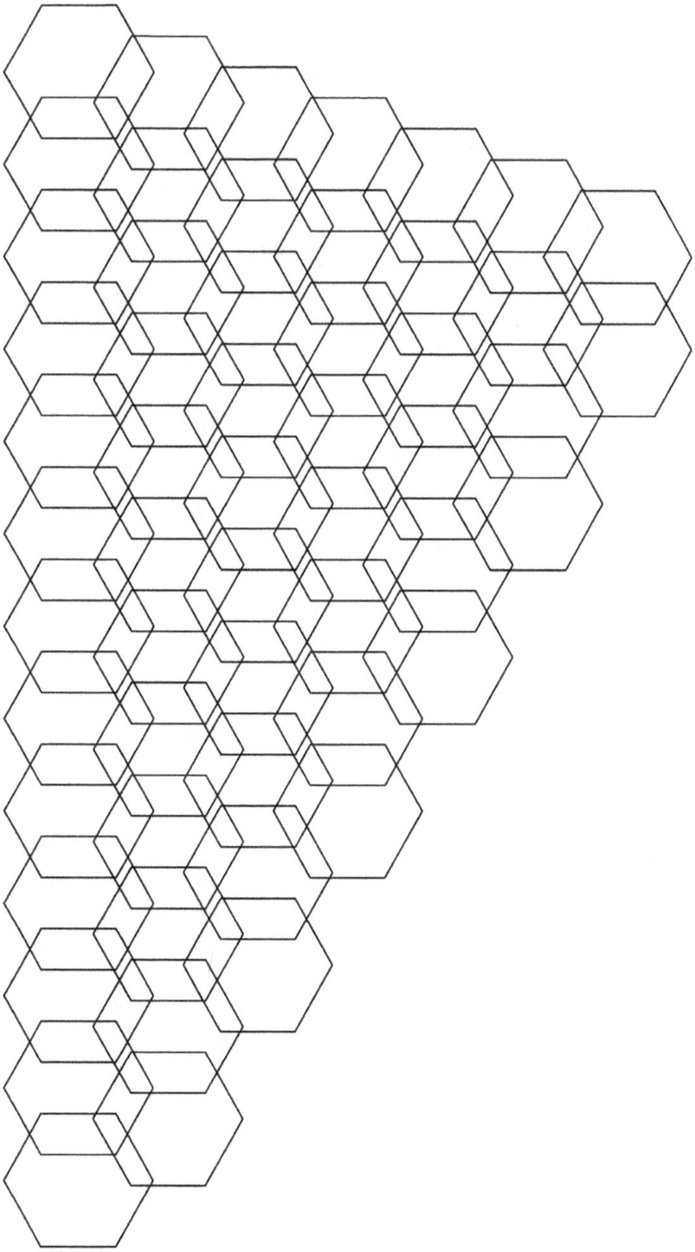

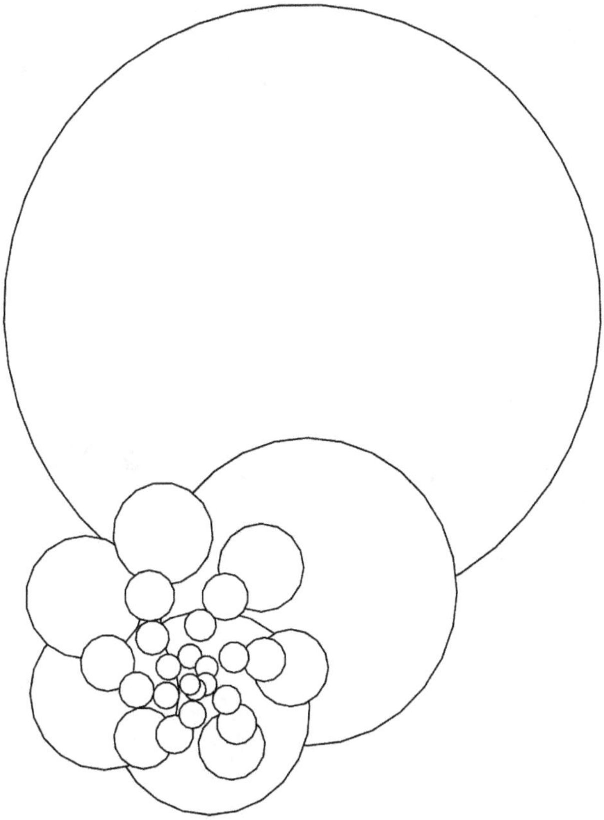

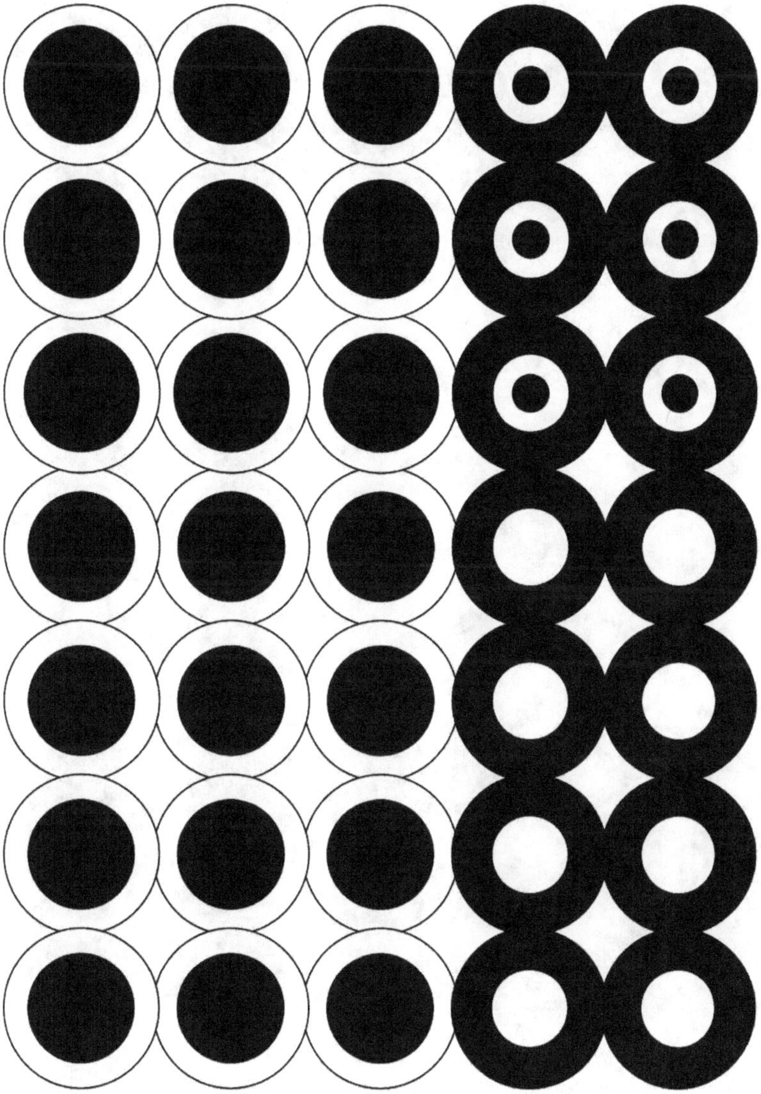

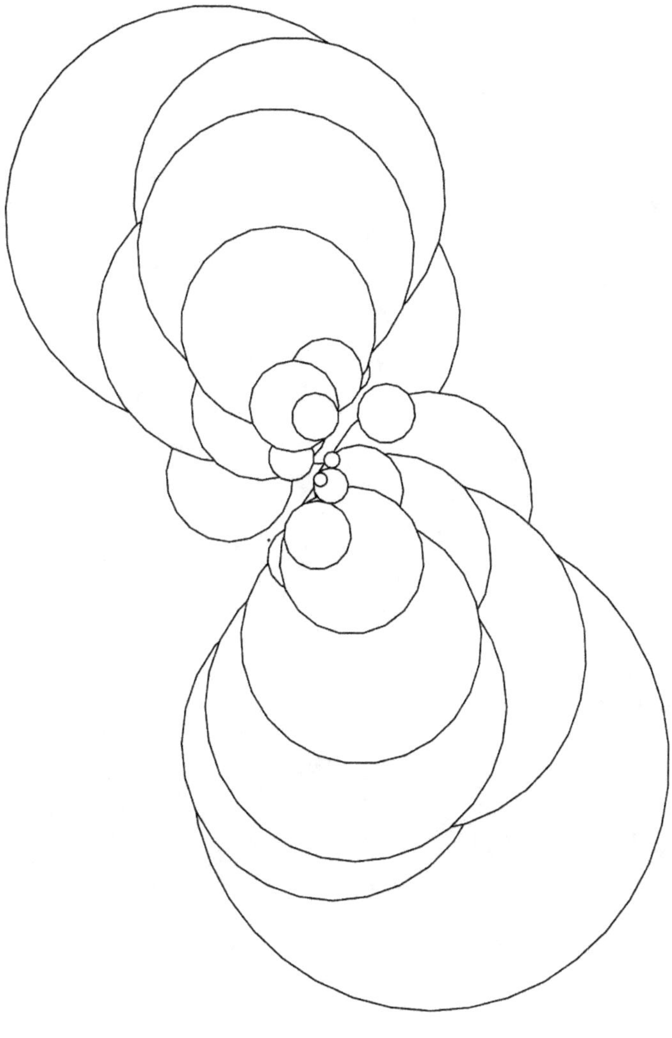

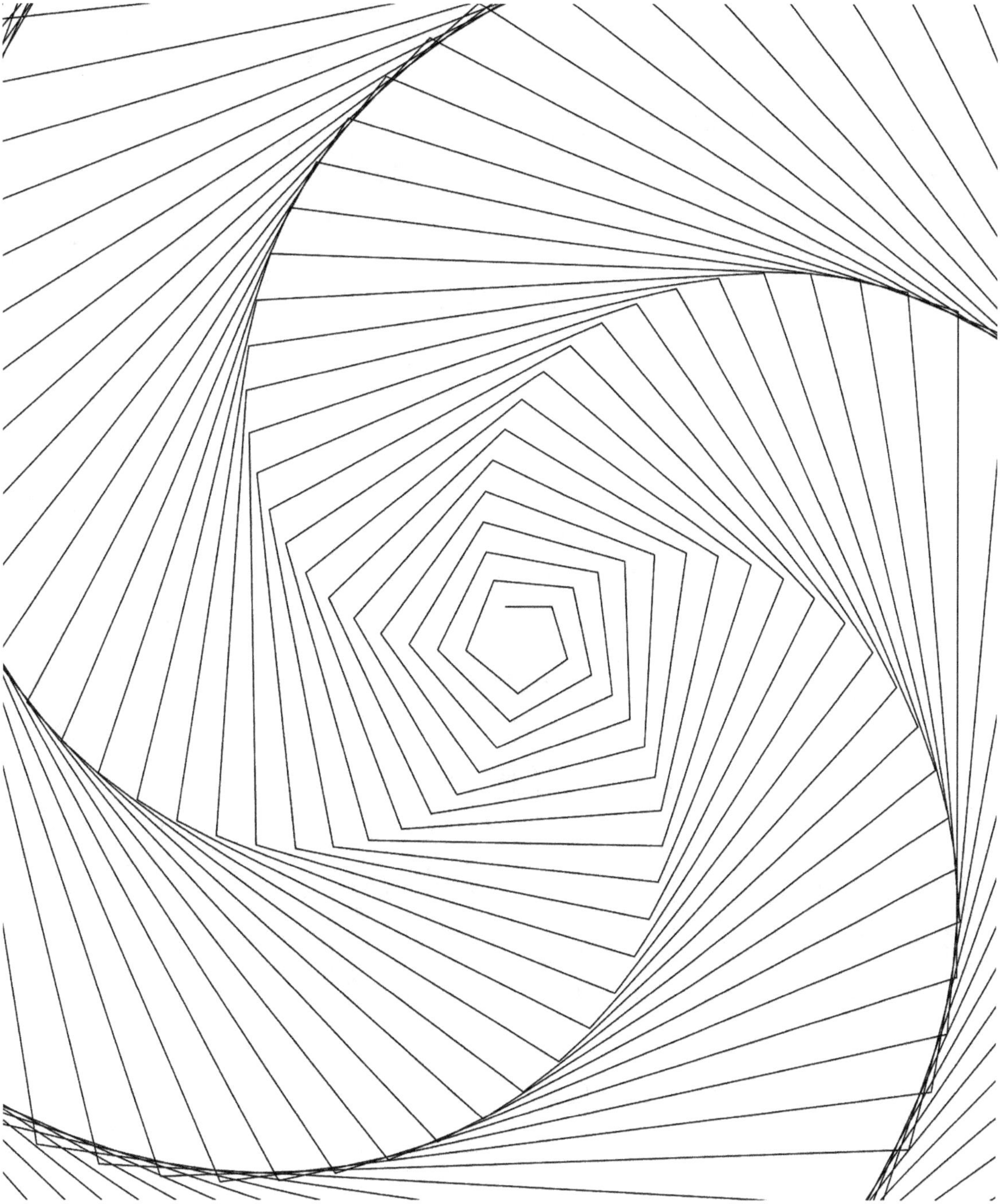

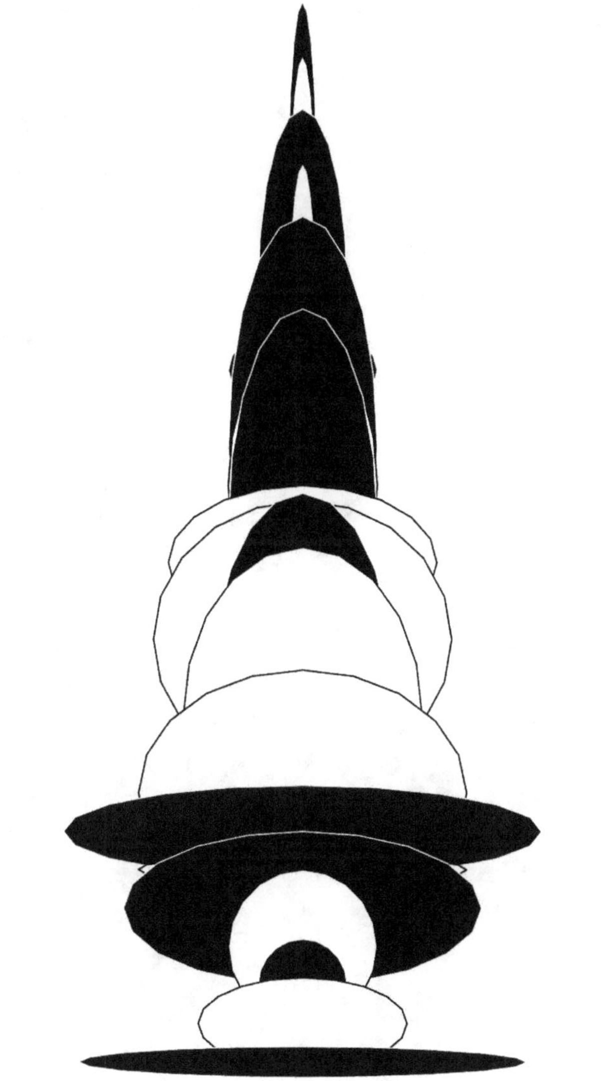

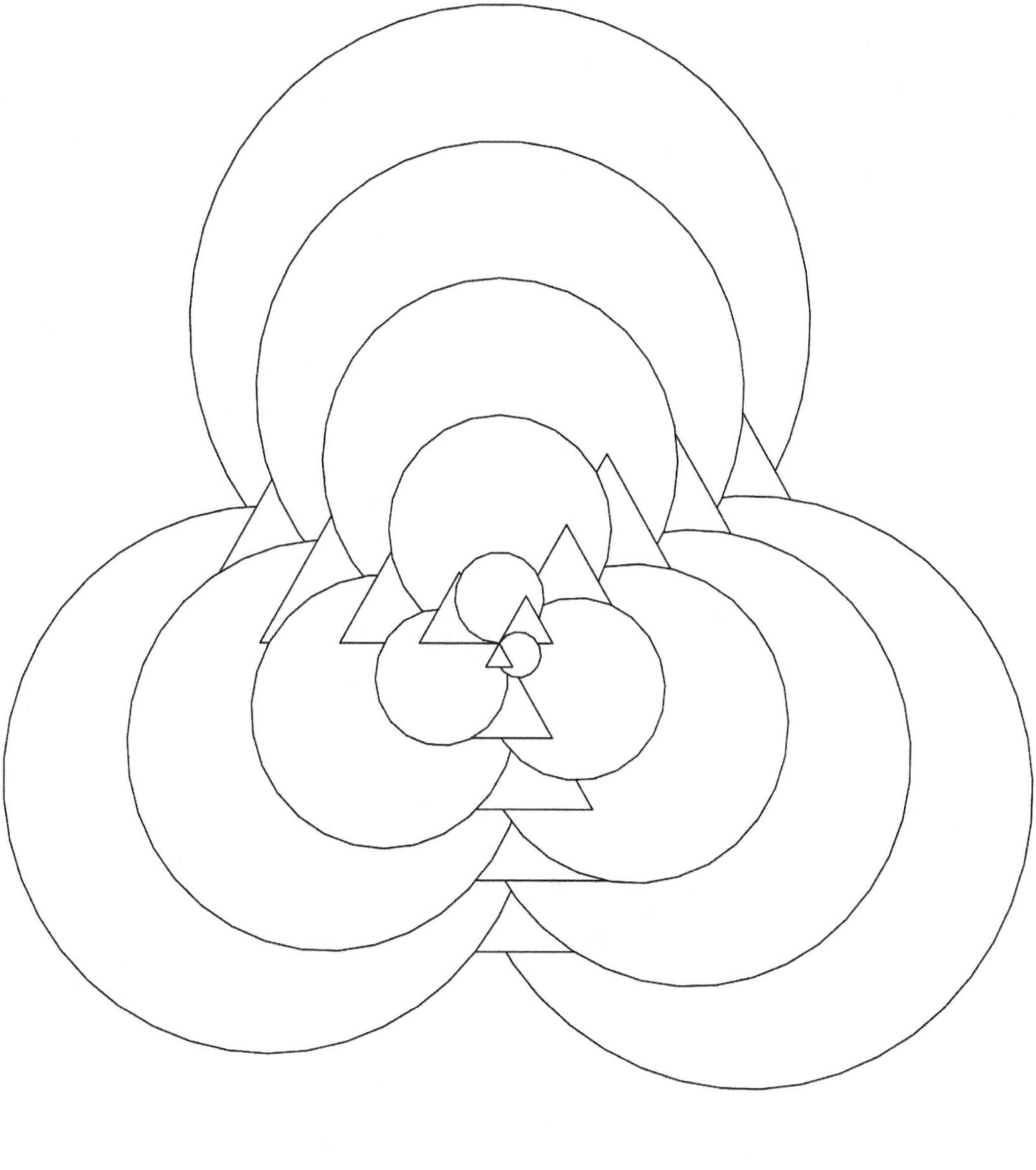

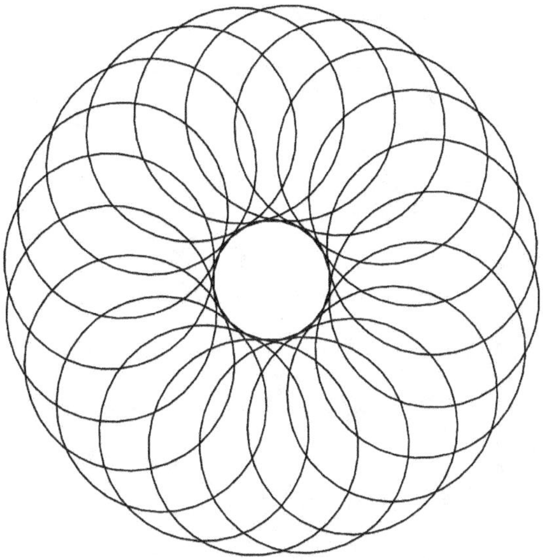

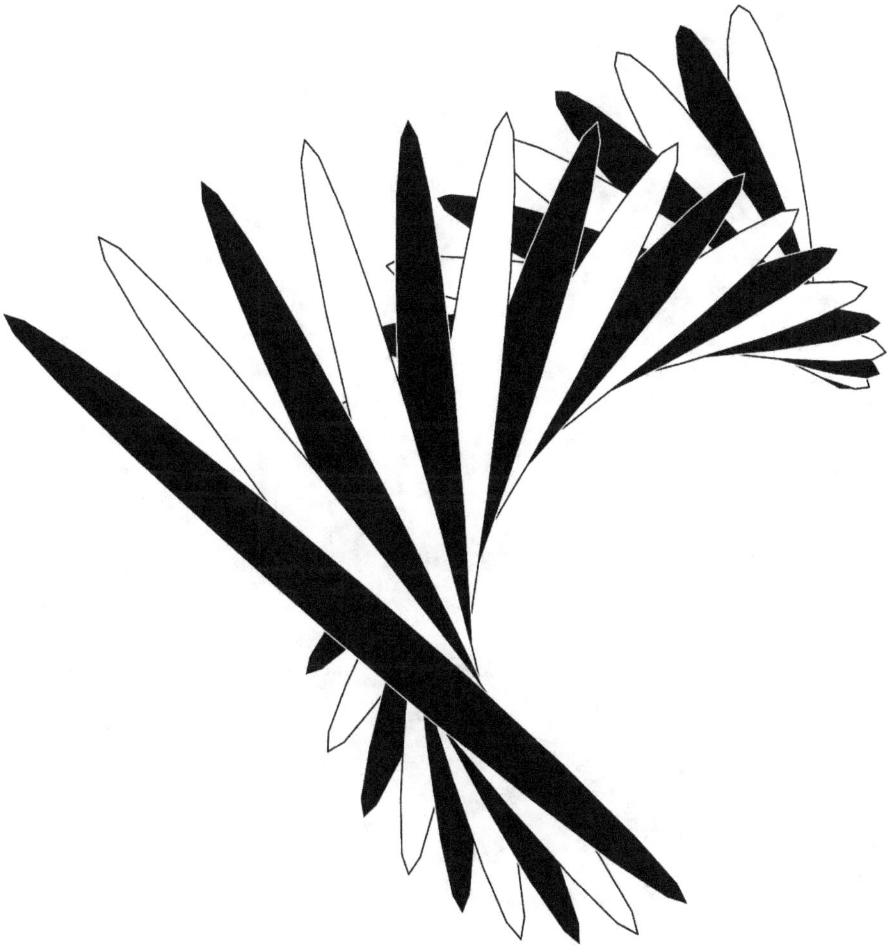

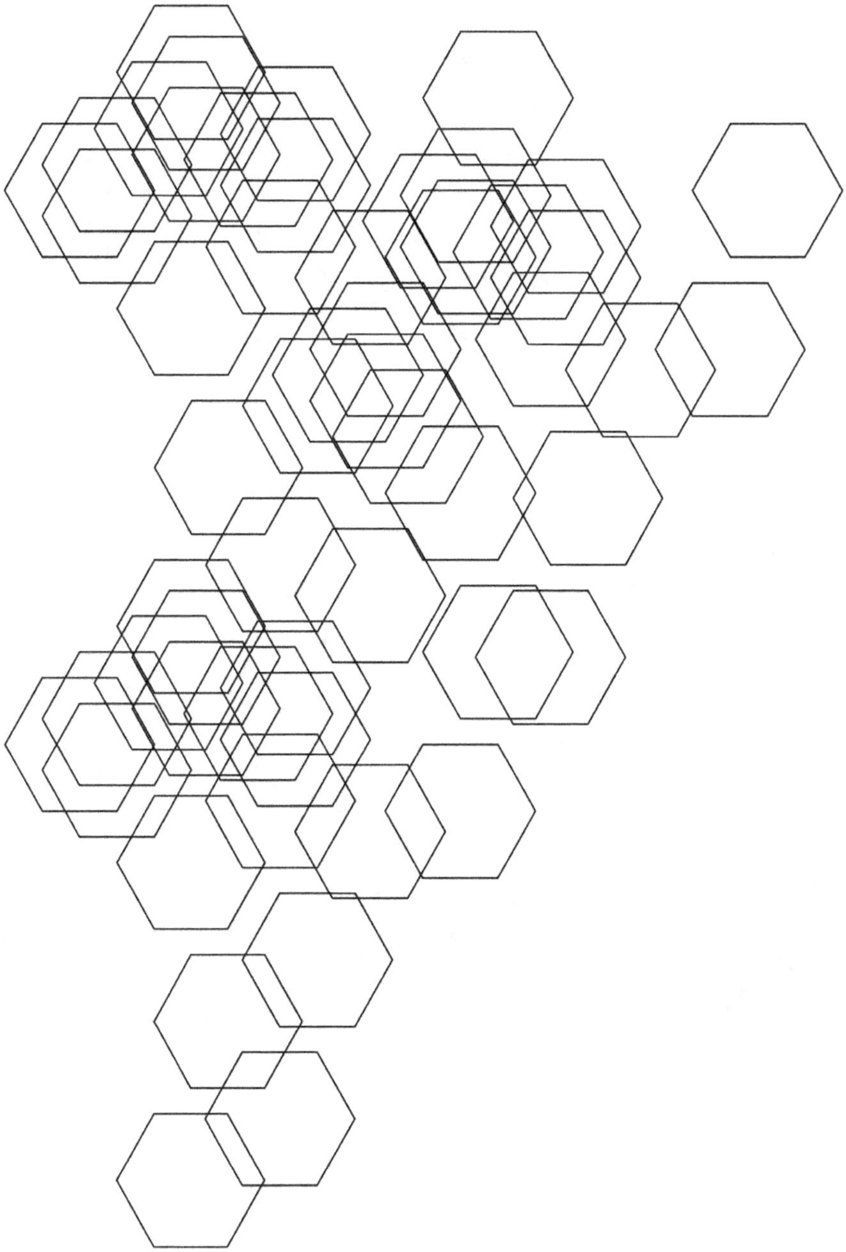

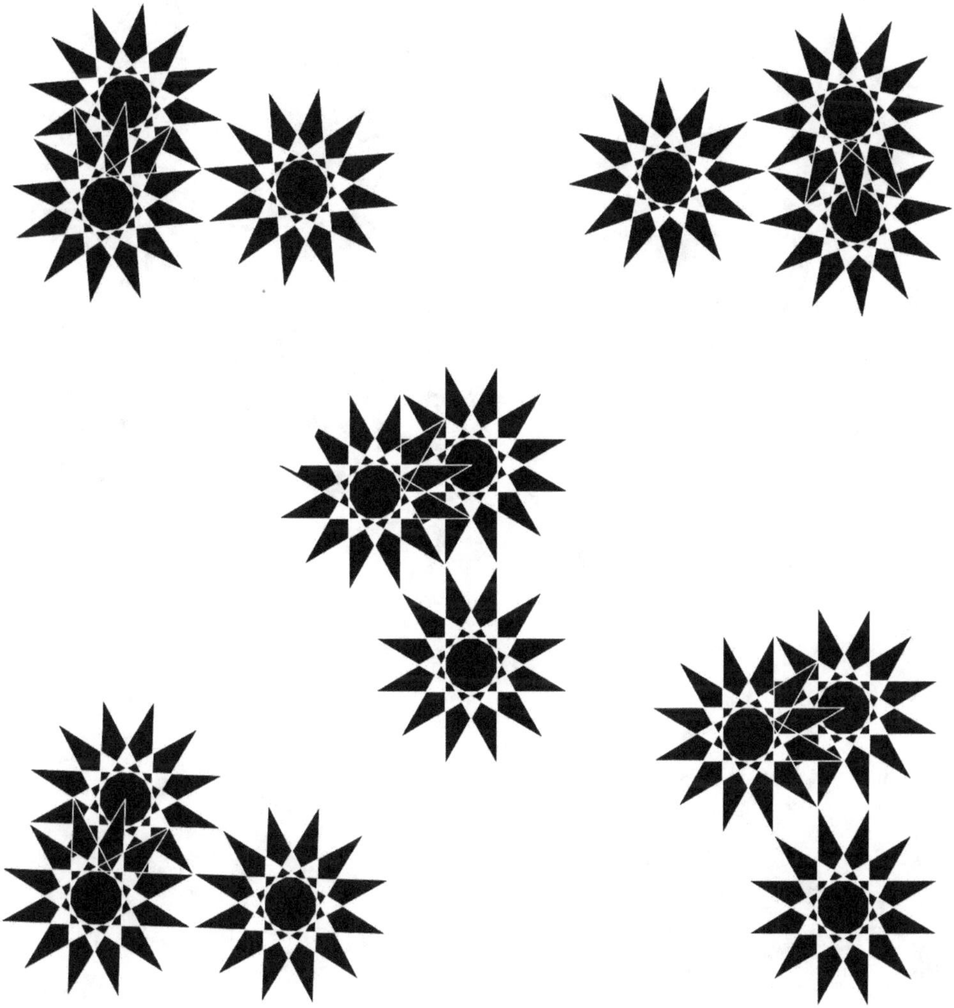

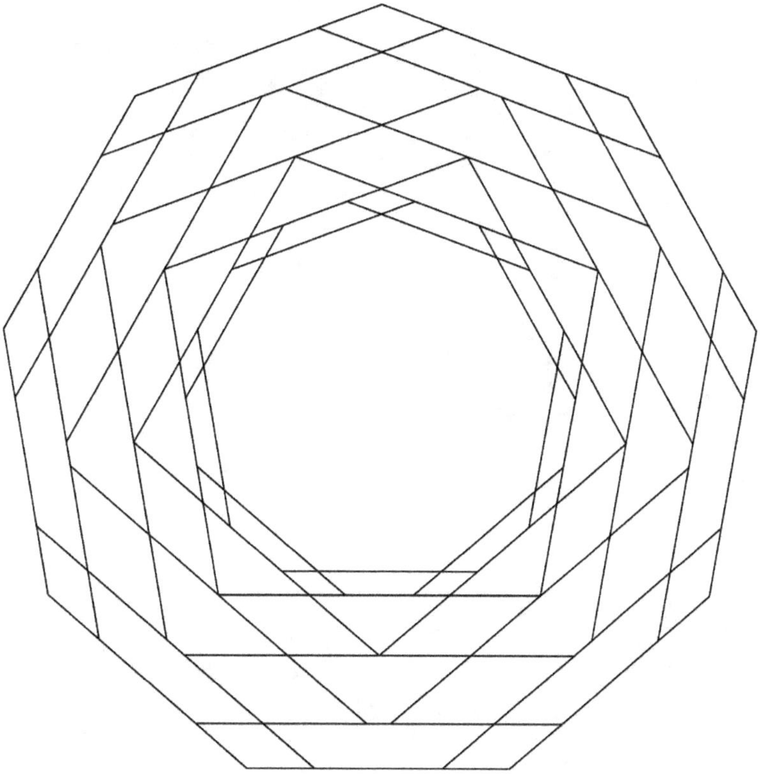

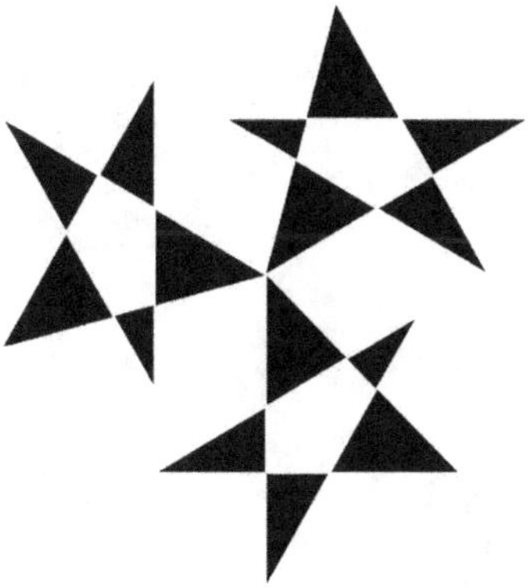

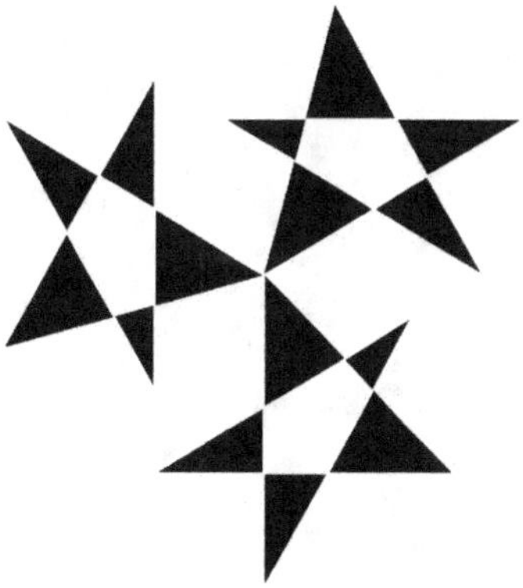

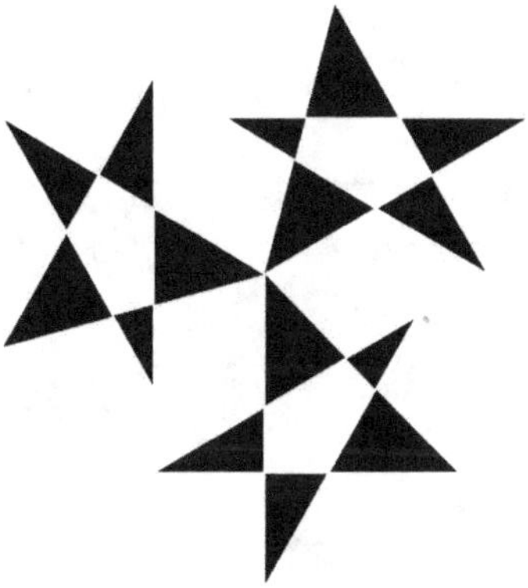

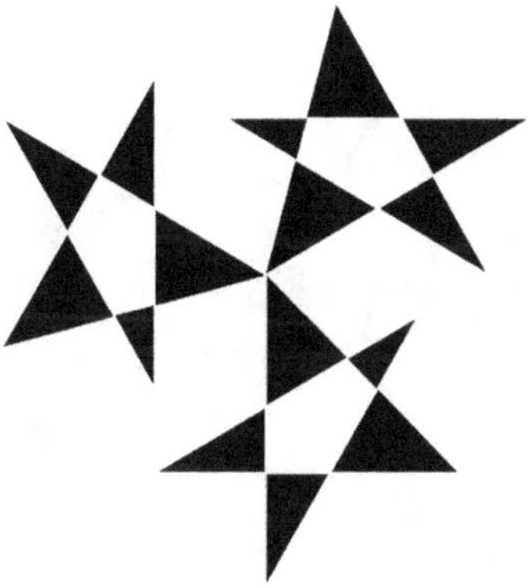

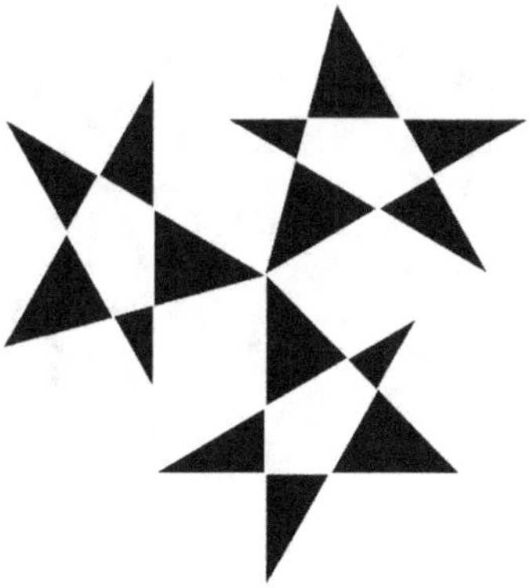

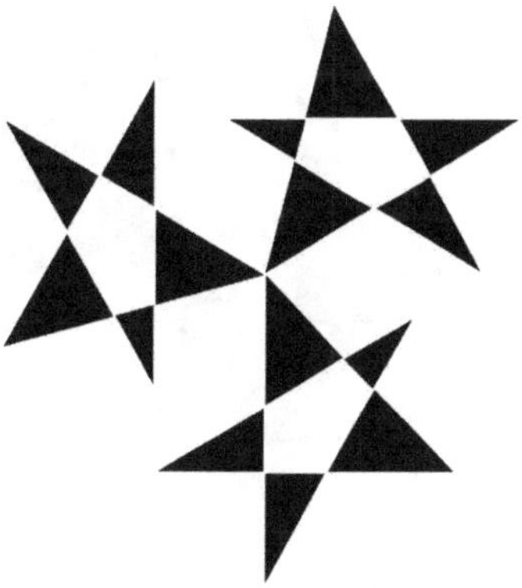

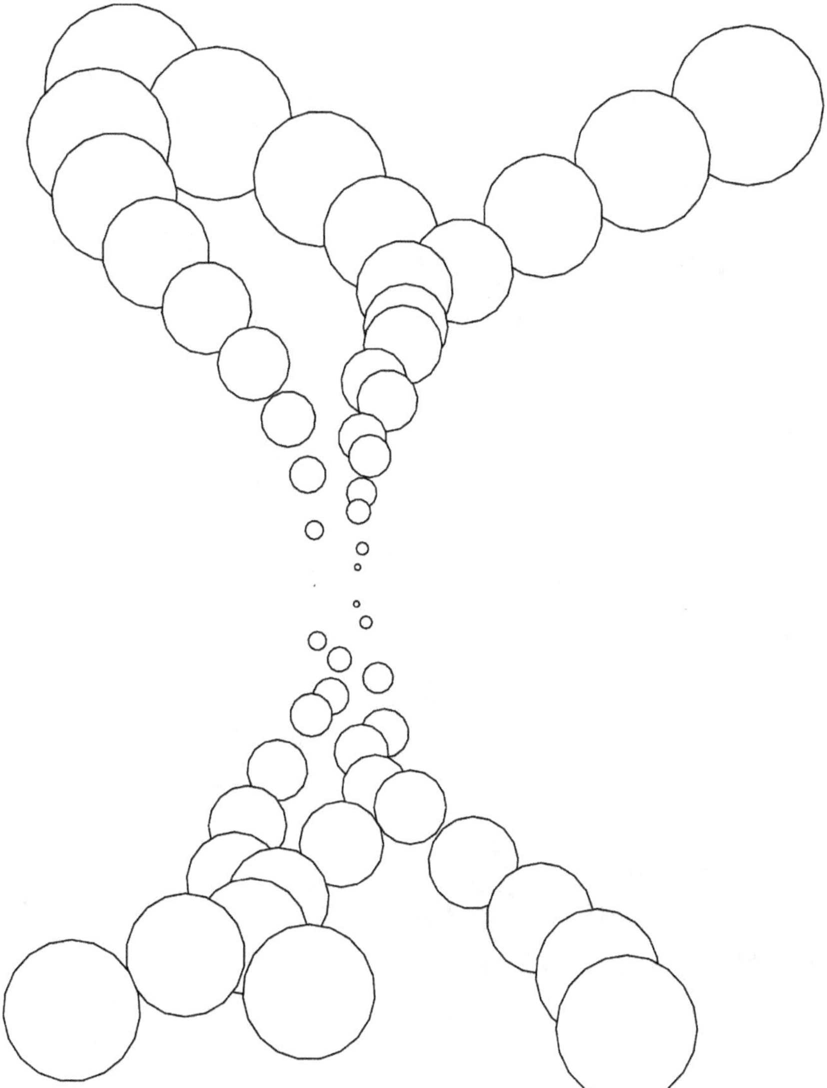

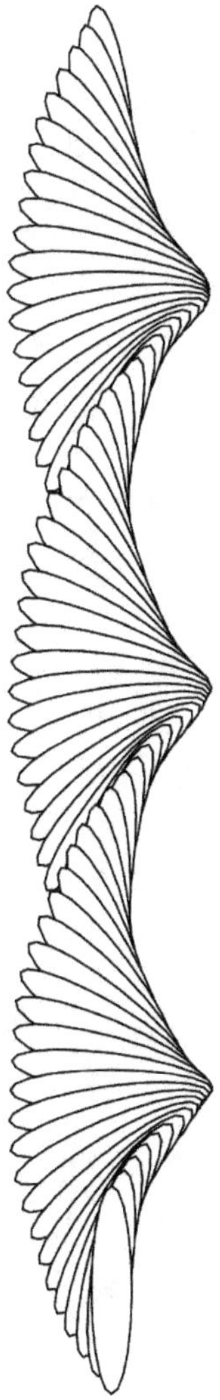

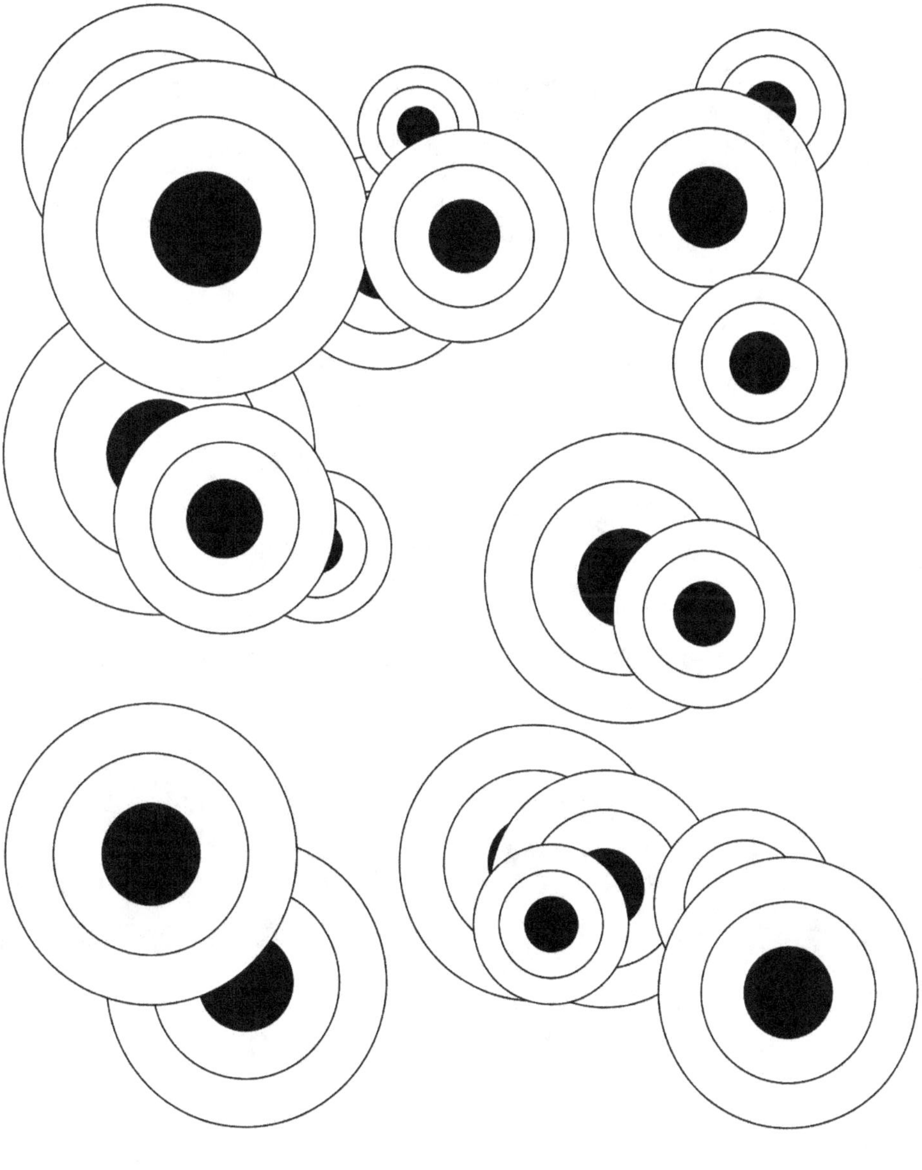

www.ingramcontent.com/pod-product-compliance
Lightning Source LLC
Chambersburg PA
CBHW081739220526
45468CB00008B/2168
9781723379710